The Infinite Artist

DOUGLAS PAUL SMITH

ISBN: 978-1-7335708-1-7

First Edition: December, 2018

Publisher: Divine Creativity Publishing, Ojai, CA, 2018

For information contact: info@divinecreativity.org

or go to www.divinecreativity.org

Cover Design and Interior Design: Douglas Paul Smith

Cover image: *Tomb of the Diver*, (approx.470 B.C.), Public Domain. File:Paestum Taucher, Wikimedia.org

Author Photo: Marion Meister

Editors: Marion Meister, Edward Levy, Bets Greer, Jen Tan, Amy Wallace for Marion

Contents

The Infinite
Artist

Foreword

I imagine that since you picked up this book you've already discovered that you have an innate passion to create – a distinct drive for giving the world something it does not yet have. And I would like to think that you have been wildly successful with your artistic enterprise, but maybe that is not the case. Personally, I have found that life as an artist is not so easy. As a painter, or dancer, or musician, or whatever medium it is that we choose to work in, our process can often seem like an uphill battle. So many of us have not been able to meet our own expectations, not to mention the expectations of others. If we get turned down enough times by the outside world, we tend to lose hope and confidence in becoming what we thought we were destined to be.

As for the realities of living as an artist, some of us have jobs that don't lend us enough time or energy to follow our creative urges. We often don't have the space to create in, or the right connections with the right people. Many of us weren't selected by the art schools we applied to. Or we did study art in college, but dropped out for whatever reason. Some of us ended up studying something else that other people, like our parents, wanted us to study so we could get a job, support ourselves, and live a logical, sensible life. Some of us did all of that, and now we're looking back thinking, 'why did I do that?' There could be hundreds of reasons why we are not doing the thing we really feel called to do. Yet there is something inside of us still waiting to be born, to be set free into this world.

So then, what happens when you don't answer the call? Perhaps you live with the underlying sense that something is missing from your life. Maybe you work a day job that you dread, but you don't leave because the world runs on money — you settle because you are sick of struggling. Maybe you have anxiety issues, or you've developed health problems that never seem to get better. It's possible that you are depressed and have a rough time getting out of bed in the morning. Or maybe you joined a spiritual group of some kind and began hiding yourself in dull states of 'meditation,' praying for the absolute to come so you can dissolve yourself into it and never return.

I have known many artists, including myself, who let their fears get the best of them, who were depressed, or anxious, doing things like overeating, abusing drugs, or getting into unhealthy, unsustainable relationships, and not knowing why they were doing it. Maybe that is you.

I must tell you — if so, you are not alone. What I have come to know is that when we don't do our creative life's work, follow our joy, live out our true purpose, calamity follows us around like a stray puppy. The excitement of life smolders. And we, the artists, know exactly what stops us from stepping up to the plate and playing ball: fear.

And our fear, at its core, might look like this: we are afraid of breaking the traditions created by our fellow humans who have decided the arts are not that important. The mind is a monkey, as they say in the meditation traditions of Asia. And we are card-carrying members of a monkey-minded society that share an unwritten agreement: we must accept the system, and we must do what is 'right' by others – our parents, our siblings, our teachers, our friends and neighbors – at the expense of following our own true calling.

As we swing along with the flow of the familiar crowd through a consensus-driven, systematized way of life, we might have the nagging feeling that we've sold ourselves as slaves to something we don't quite understand. Many artists, without finding much cultural or financial support, have relinquished their dreams for a numbed-down facsimile of artistic expression in the form of, for example, corporate advertising design and brand identity. So many of us have resigned ourselves to becoming cogs in the hamster wheel of capitalist success. Now, as we look back, our guts ache, and we have the sneaking suspicion that we may have accidentally drunk the Kool-Aid.

It is no measure of health to be well adjusted to a profoundly sick society.

— Jiddu Krishnamurti

The path of the artist is inherently a spiritual one. It has never been a path that assumes conventional or standardized roles, because the nature of it is exploratory, both of the physical and nonphysical. As I'm sure you know, this is why it's so difficult to work in a corporate or factory job if you have deep, creative passions. We artists are not systematizers – we are not really interested in default ways of thinking and being, or of acting as mass-production generators. On the contrary, our fascination lies in the mystery of creation and the hidden secrets offered up through the body and mind.

And so, any sensitive individual suffers from the current state of cultural affairs because they know that something is lacking. As in T.S. Eliot's 'The Waste Land,' so many of us have become disconnected from the truest part of ourselves – and dried out:

> *A heap of broken images, where the sun beats,*
> *And the dead tree gives no shelter, the cricket no relief,*
> *And the dry stone no sound of water.*

The good news is, with a little help from those who have been through the worst of it, we can find water again. There is a way, dear Artist, for you to get back on your feet, and be happy doing what you were born to do.

CHAPTER

One

The Artist's Dilemma

I want to say to all the creatives who have been taught to believe who you are is not enough for this world, taught that a life of art will amount to nothing, know that who we are, and what we do is life. When we create, we are creating the world. Remember this, and commit.

— Nayyirah Waheed

DEAR ARTIST,

I WANT TO WALK YOU THROUGH A DREAM I HAD RECENTLY. IMAGINE:

YOU ARE ON AN OCEAN LINER IN THE MIDDLE OF THE OCEAN. IT IS COLD OUT AND THE SKY IS DARK. YOU PEER OUT A PORTHOLE OF THE DINING HALL, AND WATCH AS THE MAMMOTH SHIP FLOATS

DANGEROUSLY CLOSE TO DARKENED SHAPES OF ROCK THAT JUT OUT FROM THE TINY WAVES BELOW.

Suddenly you hear a bang. The floor beneath you shudders, and you see people stumble, trying to maintain their balance. Panic ensues. Within minutes, the floor boards begin to tilt and the whole room turns slowly to meet the pull of gravity. Unable to bear the screaming and chaos, you run for the starboard deck. A quick glance verifies all the life boats are full beyond capacity. As you cringe at the distant sound of cracking steel and wood, the stark reality settles in. This is the moment you must make a choice that will result in either life, or death.

Your whole body becomes stiff with a palpable fear. As you gaze out into the stars, then peer down into the icy waves, you imagine the terror of going down with the ship, getting sucked into the black swirl of death. You are left standing there motionless, wrapped in a baffled state of indecision.

Out of nowhere, without thought, your last hope becomes clear: you must jump.

You scramble for a spot on the deck that promises a fair landing. As you climb onto the icy deck rails, your bones begin to shrink in frozen anticipation of this suicidal act. One last hesitation emerges – a dream of warmth and sunlight that resonates through your body – a hope that light-filled angels will appear and lift you up above to the safety of the clouds. Then, finally, you resign, and let yourself fall into the abyss.

You hear a crash but don't feel anything. When you open your eyes, to your astonishment you are still here. But something is quite different. Somehow your body knows how to move through the water, and an unseen force is helping you breathe. You are flooded with a sudden, unexpected feeling of joy as you begin to propel yourself with ease through the clear ocean depths into the unknown. Seeing more clearly than ever before, you gaze at the wavering, golden lights peering out from the rock formations beneath you. Bright blue and yellow fish swim around in all directions. A silent, yet familiar melody animates your soul. Everything feels surreal, yet very...right.

In this new world, you are perfectly supported – perhaps more peaceful and happy than you have ever been. You ponder, how could this be? Without your knowing why, there is an incredible, oceanic feeling that you have finally come home.

* * *

I thought it might be interesting for you to know, dear Artist — when I started out as a visual artist in my early 20's, my life was the Titanic. Everything I had planned was sinking into a black swirl of death. I hated my job, I couldn't stay in college, and my relationships didn't work out. As the sea of my confusion threatened to engulf me, it became clear that I had to abandon life as I knew it and take a leap into the unknown. So I started to paint.

Later on, I came to the realization that this wasn't much of a choice. Regardless of how I decided to live out my life, it seemed I had been assigned by some larger force, a mission to create art — to express some deep yearning for something unseen that was inside me.

When I first took that leap, my drive to create came from

that deep yearning as well as from the expectations of others, which basically amounted to, 'Ok, let's see those paintings you keep talking about, bro.' I didn't realize until after having lost my creative compass over and over again that in order to keep painting I had to have an internal agreement with myself that I was going to do it. And for that I had to know why I was doing it.

And why was I doing it? I honestly didn't really know. Many years went by before I finally grokked that creating art was the truest act I could perform in this life. Once I discovered this, I was much more able to focus on honing my creative process. What happened after that was that everything in my life got better. I felt more like myself – I felt free. I didn't have to try to think so much anymore, I could just let go of the details of life and let things fall into place by themselves. The world seemed to want to support me somehow, without my knowing why.

The object isn't to make art. It's to be in that wonderful state that makes art inevitable.

— Robert Henri

You could say the inevitability of art is what I discovered, and it is what this book is about. Once we artists find our way through the forest to this golden path, we hold the key to the palace. We have a way to give our life meaning, to take us out of our conditioned roles into something greater and more connected to what we truly are. We have a tool we can use to shape our lives, to focus or to broaden our experience beyond the confines of our supposed limitations.

Contrary to what I presumed for many years, the creative act is not really something that we do. It is a process of energy transformation, guided by the thread of our intentions, that ends up as something physical or vibrational. When we genuinely make art, we are not actually doing the doing of it. We are releasing ourselves into the natural momentum of the already expanding, self-generating universe. We're letting ourselves in on the magic.

But this letting-go process takes work for most of us because we are wired to want to hold on — to things, to ideas, to our deeply held beliefs. And any attempt at forcing the letting-go process becomes a contradiction, never really working out for us the way we imagined it would. So herein lies the artist's dilemma. And to add to our pickle, there is no instruction manual to go along with it. No roadmap, no tour guide, no Jedi Master. If we're lucky or persistent enough we can find direction in a good teacher, or in going to an art school we like. But ultimately we have to find this path on our own.

I thought there was someone who could tell me how to paint a landscape. But I never found that person. I had to just settle down and try. I thought someone could tell me how but I found nobody could. They could tell you how they painted their landscape. But they couldn't tell me how to paint mine.

— Georgia O'Keeffe, By Myself, BBC Documentary, 2016

CHAPTER

Two

How I Learned to Swim

The climb might be tough and challenging, but the view is worth it. There is a purpose for that pain, you just can't always see it right away.

— Victoria Arlen

Dear Artist,

I want to tell you more of my back story, to give you a better picture of who I am and why I am writing this book.

My journey through the jungle of creative learning has been a long one. As a kid I remember making drawings with crayons and markers that my mother had mailed away to a company.

The drawings came back eternalized onto plastic dinner plates. I remember being so proud of those plates when we ate off of them at Thanksgiving — they seemed so official, like beautiful, white, framed works of art. That I was able to express my innermost thoughts and be able to have other people see them, and even eat off of them, was unfathomably blissful.

Since I didn't have any art teachers growing up, I just drew whatever came out of me, following my imagination, going to places I couldn't go with my body. In junior high and high school I experimented a lot with different media, making model airplanes, doing big paper mache figures, making videos, playing the drums, and making sculptures out of whatever materials I could find. Then in college I decided to go through an Industrial Design program, thinking I could combine my creativity with something that would earn a good living, appease my family and impress my friends. But after a couple years of long nights in the design studio I became disenchanted with the idea of designing products that would simply become another brick in the wall of a capitalist consumer system I didn't believe in. It just didn't feel right to me. It didn't fit in with my deepest ideals about how I was going to make the world a better, more harmonious place.

So after I gave up on formal education, I started to do what I had done since childhood that came from a place deep inside of me and wanted to express itself. I got serious about it, painting more and more, then started showing my work in local cafés. Everything was great, but I wasn't selling my paintings. I loved what I was doing but I didn't know why people weren't buying them. Nonetheless, I kept at it, working different jobs to support myself while continuing to paint.

Making and selling paintings became an obsession for me, but as it wasn't working out the way I expected, I looked for ways in which I could draw and illustrate for publications and production companies. I went through various roles where I felt I could be creative and make money at the same time, but was never really satisfied, because those jobs didn't allow for true expression – they somehow felt stifling and unnatural. Again, they seemed to be more about selling things, and had little to do with what I believed making art was really about. After I finally graduated from college, I made enough money from odd jobs to get a tiny 10x15-foot room in an artist community building in downtown Seattle. I started painting every day – it was easy because I met friends there who were doing it too – and it felt so great just to commit fully to doing my work. But painting full time brought up so much energy and emotion in me that I became unbalanced and started smoking and drinking a lot to compensate.

Though I sold a lot of paintings, earning more money than I had previously, so much partying led to unforeseeable problems. I broke up with my girlfriend, my health started to suffer, and it became obvious that this wasn't a sustainable lifestyle. So I got a job doing carpentry, got pretty good at it, and made my living that way for some time. This was fine, but I still knew I had to make paintings.

For many years I went back and forth, working a day job and then quitting so I could paint for a while, then getting another job after my exhibition. But I could never reconcile the two. Working for other people paid my bills, gave me character and put hair on my chest, but it rarely seemed to give me enough time or energy to do my creative work. And when I was able to do my creative work, I often felt I was doing it just to sell paintings and keep my style consistent with the market so I could sell more. I was doing it for all the wrong reasons, and so it stopped being a fun, natural process. This eventually wore me down, and I stopped painting altogether.

For a long time, I couldn't figure out what was wrong with me. I kept thinking, maybe it's my Midwestern Protestant guilt, or it's generations of family shame unknowingly passed down to me. I tried reading self-help books. Nothing changed. Then I had a nervous breakdown, followed by severe, ongoing illnesses. I developed strange binge-eating habits, and became so depressed I couldn't sleep at night. I saw a psychologist for a few years, followed by a multitude of doctors and healers, for another 12 years. No one seemed to know what was wrong with me, physically or mentally, and nothing I tried was helping; my health became a constant battle.

Meanwhile, I started getting into Buddhist meditation and philosophy to try and see why life wasn't working out. This was an exciting time, because I was learning things they never taught me in high school or college, like how my mind works, and how we create our own reality, mostly unconsciously, because we're not being present in our lives. I started meditating every day for hours. Then I gave away all my belongings and packed up my car and drove to the desert to join a Tibetan Buddhist university. I was hungry for answers, so in addition to that I began exploring other traditions of Buddhism and other forms of Eastern spirituality, like yogic philosophy and Taoism. Eventually, I found the teachings of Chögyam Trungpa, who seamlessly fit together a lot of the missing pieces of my puzzle. By combining the Zen traditions of contemplative art with Tibetan Buddhist meditation and ancient Taoist principles, Trungpa came up with a system of creative learning that focused entirely on the process of creation, instead of the product. It seemed to give answers to some of my deepest questions – what is creativity, really, and why are we compelled to create? And how do I do it consistently in a way that supports a deeper yearning for truth? And, how can I live even a marginally happy life in a world that seems to be going to pieces all around me, when I have no control over it? I was so elated to find Trungpa's teachings – I dove into them and experimented with them in my painting and other creative practices. Ultimately, these became the basis for many of the practices in this book.

After I went through my teacher training in Trungpa's system, I began teaching and experimenting with my own version, calling it 'Art as Meditation.' I did this on and off for years while working even more odd jobs. I continued my meditation practice and spiritual seeking, finding answers to questions from various traditions and methodologies, for another decade.

Eventually, thanks to my teachers and a good amount of trial and error, I got to a point of consistent peace and clarity, and a deep understanding of how my state of mind affects my reality. I realized that being a healthy person with healthy relationships had nothing to do with other people or with working really hard at something – it was, ultimately, about overcoming my own self-hatred and self-sabotaging by changing my worldview, and by staying connected to something bigger than myself. In the end, I discovered that becoming a truly happy person was actually doable, and that it had everything to do with following my true purpose: creating art and teaching artists.

Looking back, it has been a long, windy road through the university of hard knocks. One thing I can tell you, with absolute certainty, is that you don't have to listen to all the lies about being unable to follow your art dreams because of this or that reason. You don't have to believe you are somehow unworthy of making great work, or that you have to starve to do what you love – that you must lead a life of poverty and struggle because that is somehow your fate as 'artist.'

That is not your fate as artist. Our fate as artists is nothing but our willingness to follow our intuitive desires, to expand our awareness into other ways of being. That doesn't mean we have to give up the rest of our lives and become the next Jeff Koons in order to be happy or to fulfill our earthly purpose. It doesn't have to be so all-or-nothing. It can just be very simple and straightforward, very divinely, beautifully ordinary. What I'm suggesting is, I don't believe that you have to suffer some great trial to get to where you want to be with your art. My intention with this book is not just to make it realistic for you, but imminent.

CHAPTER
Three

Your True Purpose: Following the Artist's Path

Something inside me has always been there. But now it's awake...and I'm afraid. I don't know what it is, or what to do with it, and I need help.

— Rey from Jakku, Star Wars Episode VIII, The Last Jedi

Dear Artist,

One thing I know for certain is that life is not about working your ass off in some mind-numbing job for 40 years, paying taxes, retiring, having a cocktail, and dying. We artists are the one percent who have a purpose here that does not involve orthodox roles like climbing the corporate ladder, or dropping bombs on people, or hoarding money, or trying to have power over other human beings in some way.

✳ We have the opportunity to become visionaries, bright reflectors, pioneers of culture. Many of us, it seems, have been born with the capacity for great understanding and positive change. We have a deep sensitivity and connection with the truth of things. We know that the world can become a place in which all humans and all other beings can not only survive, but thrive, for no other reason than this: we are here experiencing the miracle of life on planet Earth, so why not make it good?

Many of us feel that we were born with a mission. And that mission often has something to do with our bliss, like how angels have bliss, flying around and helping other beings – or like how scuba divers have bliss, exploring the vast depths of the world undersea. Some artists might have a mission to make giant paintings and have people be inspired by them, or buy them for lots of money so they can make even more paintings, or explore other fun options of creating. And their impetus for wanting to do this might be that they are connected to a mysterious place inside of them that wants to inspire the world; to show others that they can see things in a different light, or live in a more expansive, connected way.

The Artiste Manqué

I'm confident that, since you are reading this, you have some kind of understanding about the importance of your own mission – that it's not just some trivial thing that you can just decide to do or not to do, for whatever reason. I'm guessing you have already sensed, and even experienced, that your creative impulse is part of something bigger than your rational mind lets on. You might have intuited that your role in this life has a quality similar to what is known in the Indian spiritual traditions as lila (or leela) – the sportive, spontaneous activity of Brahman, the divine source of creation. And possibly, you can see the relationship between your own creative impulses and the divine impulses that created your own body and mind – that you, yourself, create in much the same way that you were created.

Maybe you already know that taking your mission lightly just doesn't feel right. You might have sensed, somewhere in the back of your mind, that knowing about your divine path and following it are two very distinct things.

Somewhat unfortunately, our ego-driven free will, which often has its own agenda and does not listen to the wisdom of the higher self, gives us the option of looking in the other direction. If you have explored the dark, dead-end road of ignoring your higher purpose and trying to fit into a 'normal' life – then you are already familiar with the artiste manqué: one who has failed to embrace the burden of his or her difference as artist-creator.

As author Matthew Fox reveals in *Creativity*, "Every responsible artist comes to grips with his or her differentiation from others. There follows an immense feeling of guilt for 'unused life, the unlived in us,' when we fail our responsibility to give birth as we are here to do."

This consequent feeling of guilt, if left unchecked, invariably gives way to neurosis. In turning away from our life-affirming, expressive nature as creators, we begin to develop instead, life-denying patterns of emotional destructiveness and self defeat. As we suppress our emotions, trying to bottle them up, pretending it doesn't really matter, the pressure builds up. Eventually, our bottles leak out, or explode into psychological difficulties, emotional misadventures, and in many cases, physical illness.

> *If the person doesn't listen to the demands of his own spiritual and heart life and insists on a certain program, you're going to have a schizophrenic crack-up. The person has put himself off center. He has aligned himself with a programmatic life and it's not the one that the body's interested in at all. And the world is full of people who have [...] stopped listening to themselves. In my own life, I've had many opportunities to commit myself to a system, and to go with it, and to obey its requirements. My life has been that of a maverick – I would not submit.*

> — Joseph Campbell

The individual woes that come with rejecting one's greater purpose can, at times, be unbearable. They can bring out the absolute worst in us until we barely recognize ourselves. Many of us, having spent many years in these wretched states of unhappiness, have vowed never to go back.

And yet, there is another, larger problem that is born from our divergences – I wonder if you could imagine a scenario where all artists have given up their missions. Try to picture a world without Michelangelo, Picasso, Shakespeare, or Hemingway. A world without J.K. Rowling, or Maya Angelou, or Ella Fitzgerald. Envision for a moment a world without rock, classical, or jazz music. A world where people cannot think deeply, or have their own unique experiences – where personal satisfaction cannot come from the depths of our contemplation, or revelation, but only from technological advancements, capital gains, or material possessions. I wonder – what would we do with ourselves? Would we work all day long in an office, our only reward being that we get to do it all over again the next day? Would we pursue our technologies in order to become more technological, and develop our comforts for the sole purpose of becoming more comfortable?

Admittedly, our Earth is already incredibly articulate and exquisite in its ways, needing no human invention or aesthetic alteration. But we humans, being a part of nature, have been given an innate drive to warm ourselves by the fires of our imaginations, to create new life with the materials we've been given, and to share our creations with the world. Though some of us seem to have this creative urge much stronger than others, we all have it to some degree. However, it appears that many of us who have discovered it have yet to understand its significance to ourselves and to the bigger picture.

The Artist's Role as Shaman

A human being is part of the whole, called by us "universe," limited in time and space. He experiences himself, his thoughts and feelings as something separated from the rest – a kind of optical delusion of his consciousness. This delusion is a prison, restricting us to our personal desires and to affection for a few persons close to us.

Our task must be to free ourselves from our prison by widening our circle of compassion to embrace all humanity and the whole of nature in its beauty.

— Albert Einstein

The fact is, when we listen to the call of our divine assignment and take action in a certain direction, we affect not only ourselves but all those around us. We inspire others to follow their own purpose, whether or not we intend to do so.

Discoveries in quantum physics – including Einstein's theory of Quantum Entanglement, Rupert Sheldrake's Morphic Resonance theory, and most recently, Nassim Haramein's work in Unified Physics – all confirm our separateness is illusory, and that we affect each other in ways we cannot presently fathom. These modern examinations give compelling evidence to what ancient spiritual adepts in many regions of the globe have been saying for millennia — that it appears we are separate, individual beings, but ultimately we are not. As Alan Watts used to say, we are "all rays of the same sun [...] teats on the same sow."

Given this, it's evident that our expressions as artists can hold a butterfly-effect potential that stretches far beyond what we can imagine. And it suggests our responsibilities as artists may be much greater than we think. You as an artist, like the compassionate shaman, have been given the role of telling a higher truth, about humanity and about the world we live in.

> *[T]he role of the artist [is] to stretch the envelope, it's to bring*
> *the news from the edge.... The musician, the shaman, the smith,*
> *the physician – these were all originally combined, you know,*
> *because the mystery of creation and the mystery of the human*
> *body, this was all spun together. That's why when people say*
> *[...] what is the proper response to the culture crisis? I think the*
> *response is to shamanize [...] and that means to help with the*
> *healing, to explore the invisible world, and to make art.*

— Terence McKenna, "No Guru, No Method, No Teacher," Lecture, 1993

So, what do you do with this drive once you find it? Only you, of course, can follow this question to unearth the hidden layers beneath it. If you get that far, you will find, I believe, that what you've been following is a road that leads through a muddle of perplexing turns and detours, to a place of profound self-discovery. If you've ever driven a car in someplace like New York City, you'll have some idea of what I'm talking about. The street signs rarely tell you anything useful. And when you follow them, it often seems like you're going away from your destination instead of towards it. But this is your road – it was built for you. If and when you follow it with complete trust and dedication, it will lead you to untold, unimagined riches.

Chances are your health will improve. Your relationships will get better. You'll be able to give up your shrink. You'll be more grounded in who you are, more in tune with your everyday life. You will be less susceptible to getting caught up in drama. Because you have chosen to engage with your reality instead of avoiding it, even the smallest details will win your appreciation. You will become fascinated by the infinite possibilities, by the colors and textures, the lines, the spaces in the music – by the whole and its simultaneous multitude of parts. You will move from being an individual who suffers from the disconnection of modern life, to becoming a compassionate witness to the universal process; a keeper of the space in which flow the endless waters of your creations.

The creative life is a spiritual path. As much as you can, stay connected to your heart, and let your thinking mind stick to what it knows best – solving math problems, developing motor skills, and ordering pizza. Your heart, or your intuitive sense, is much better at directing you. It is your unique connection to your higher being, and therefore much wiser and more intelligent than your thinking mind will ever be. It will get you to where you want to go without sacrificing your soul, so you can create the way you need to create, and live the way you really want to live.

CHAPTER
Four

The Mission of this Book

Everyone has a purpose in life and a unique talent to give to others. And when we blend this unique talent with service to others, we experience the ecstasy and exultation of our own spirit, which is the ultimate goal of all goals.

— Kallam Anji Reddy

Dear Artist,

My goal with this book is to help you live your deepest desires. But as much as I would like to say that there is a blue pill you can take, a just-add-water, one-size-fits-all solution to your success, I cannot. This is not a step-by-step guidebook that you can follow and instantly realize your art dreams. There will never be a book like that, that actually works for you. Every artist in history who has made great art has found their own way, with a little guidance – or a lot of guidance – from peers, mentors, and teachers.

We creatives, unlike the majority of the cookie-cutter culture, have our own unique visions, processes, individual aesthetic, work environment, and audience. Because of this, it is impossible to adhere to any one system of learning in order to get to where we want to go. What we can do, is follow other people's models of success and apply them to our own processes. By adapting sound principles along with practical advice for our specific medium and goals, things will more easily fall into place.

So, what I have put together for you in this book is all of the knowledge I didn't have when I started working as a fine artist and designer. In essence, it is that there must be a foundation for personal and professional growth, and that, once that foundation is established, growth becomes a thousand times easier. Once I realized I was missing this groundwork, it took many years of trial and error as well as following a spiritual path that emphasized self-awareness and contemplation, to find it.

As I eventually learned, it's not so much about the 'what' as the 'how'. Once you learn and adapt the 'how' part to your process, there will be no stopping you, in whatever environment or medium you choose to work in.

By far, the most important lesson I want to convey is the lesson of how to get out of your own way – and that giving ourselves to our higher purpose is the most important, most blissful and most deeply rewarding thing we can do in this life. I believe that if you follow the guidance in this book with a pure heart and an open mind, you will, inevitably, accomplish that purpose. You will witness success on many levels – beyond what you ever imagined possible.

The more of your energy, and presence, you invest in your process, the faster you will see results. With results, however small, comes confidence, and in turn, a renewed faith in your process. In time you will come to see a new paradigm of living, and you will see that your art is not really separate from the rest of your life. Your art becomes the flow of your life, and life, the flow of your art.

Undoubtedly, the deep work involved here is no small undertaking. You will most likely be working with strongly ingrained habits and fears, and chances are you will experience all kinds of resistance. It's my greatest interest as an artist coach to help you work through the obstacles to your creative success, and that is why I wrote this book. If things get difficult along the way, as they are wont to do, do not be discouraged. You can always get support from a mentor or coach to get you through the tough spots. If you want to inquire about personal coaching, my contact information is located in the back of this book.

What you will find inside this book:

- A very brief history of art, and why the world so badly needs yours.

- How following your true calling will help you, and why your gift to the world is so important.

- The art of getting into your Flow, and why it's so crucial for your creative process.

- Art As Meditation and the psychology of creativity – a bird's-eye view of your monkey-mind and the necessary steps to train it.

- How to overcome the mental and emotional blocks to becoming the artist you were born to be – they are probably not what you think they are.

- Building a relationship with your intuition – aligning with your higher Self and following your natural guidance system.

- Exercises for working with stuck emotions, procrastination and fears.

- The importance of love and gratitude in your process.

- The art of discipline, and the importance of following your own rules.

- The art of breaking rules and going against the social stream – and why it's so important.

- How being yourself – your true Self, is the key to everything you desire.

- The art of redefining yourself – identifying and changing limiting beliefs.

- The key to becoming a wealthy artist, and an examination of how we view money and wealth. Practical advice for getting patrons and making sales.

- How to create a body of work you can feel good about. Honing your process, without worrying about your product.

- The common obstacles to making great art, and how to navigate them.

- The art of persistence – showing up every day and never giving up.

CHAPTER

Five

A very short History of 'Art'

The purpose of art is to lay bare the questions that have been concealed by the answers.

— James Baldwin

Dear Artist,

Before we get started with the main topics in this book, it's important to have context for our creative purpose. I've found that having at least a basic understanding of Art History is essential for this.

First of all, I should tell you – my lifelong interest in the history of art did not start off with a bang. In college, Art History class was like sitting in the nosebleed section of a baseball game where you weren't exactly sure which teams were playing. Most of the time I ended up sleeping in the back row of the auditorium, through many hours of my French Art History professor trying to read textbook lines in the dark, next to a movie screen – in his third language.

It didn't really get better from there. Critical literature about art never really had any relevance to what I saw in the physical world of art making – maybe I missed something, but it always seemed like armchair philosophy to me. I never found anyone capable of talking about the history of art with any kind of passion or deep knowledge.

Eventually, through painting, drawing, and going to museums with other artists, I came to an understanding about how art has been used by cultures and the greater significance it has for us. I started to understand that how I define art affects my relationship to it and to the process of creating it. When I define art as something necessary and sacred, my creative process becomes easier and more meaningful. I experience other people's work in a more open-minded way, seeing through eyes that aren't my own.

However, there is one question I have about art that remains — it is arguably the most fundamental, and perhaps unanswerable question: Why? Why do we humans create art? What purpose, what edification does it provide us? It's an intriguing question, because there are so many ways to address it. My suspicion is, what is behind all of our superficial reasons for the creative act, is that we cannot help ourselves – we have to do it, because it is in our nature to do it, and because the human connection to the soul cannot survive without doing it.

In his book, Creativity, Matthew Fox tells us, "We are creators at our very core. Only creating can make us happy, for in creating we tap into the deepest powers of self and universe and the Divine Self."

It's certainly gratifying to think about a collective, spiritual purpose in the creation of art. And I think it's also fascinating to look at how art's purpose has evolved through the ages. The following is an extremely brief overview of how, and why, humans created art over time. It will give us a bird's-eye view on ourselves as artists in the 21st century.

Art Throughout the Millennia

I wonder if you have seen the Neanderthal hand-stencil paintings in the caves of Maltravieso, Spain, dated at 66,700 years old. When I look at photos of them, I become speechless. I have no idea what they mean or why they were created, yet they exude a timeless, life affirming quality that I often do not see in contemporary art.

Additionally, many of the art relics created by our more recent tribal ancestors in North and South America are equally timeless. But we know more about them, such as how their art was used in shamanic rites to explore the unseen worlds. Native American paintings of animals suggest how they viewed their hunting rituals — they were not just interested in documenting the hunt in an objective, material way. Their art was also about connecting to the spirits of the animals they hunted. It displayed their utter appreciation for and awe of life beyond what they saw with their physical eyes.

In other areas of the globe, such as ancient Greece, the awe of life was often expressed through the concept of *Arete* – the highest potential and effectiveness a human being can aspire to. Art in that time was sponsored by the government and displayed publicly to imbue its citizens with this principle. Yet we have evidence that Greek art was not concerned solely with refined anthropomorphic representation and human aspirations. It was also made for religious purposes, as sculptures were often created to represent the gods they worshipped, as well as being thought of as containing the spirits of those gods.

In other places such as on the Asian subcontinent, religious themes also played an important role in the creation of art. For thousands of years Buddhist statues and paintings were exhibited in monasteries to inspire peace and introspective awareness in monks. In India, through a ritual process, statues of deities and gurus were "enlivened" and thereafter considered to be inhabited by the actual deity, and were dressed and fed. All the while, in Europe, paintings of the Virgin Mary, the crucified Jesus, and the Pietà filled Christians with a sense of theistic faith and longing, inspiring them to follow the way of Christ.

In addition to having spiritual value, we understand that art has been used politically as the bullhorn of cultural supremacists. Many rulers, from Alexander the Great to Napoleon, commissioned visual art for the purpose of propaganda, as well as ostentatious displays of power, wealth, and status. In the 19th and 20th centuries, following the Industrial Revolution, Proletarian leaders such as Mao Zedong insisted that art and literature be used exclusively as cogs in the machine of the communist revolution. Not unlike this, modern political organizations have been known to routinely use art and design to engage constituents and bolster their campaigns.

L'Art pour L'Art

In Europe, during the early 19th Century, something fascinating happened to the popular assignment of art. The French philosopher Victor Cousin, echoing the beliefs held by many artists and writers of this new epoch, allegedly coined the term 'l'art pour l'art' – meaning 'art for the sake of art.' What he implied was that art no longer needed justification. It didn't need to be moral or didactic. It didn't have to serve some other end like politics or religion for its creation; it could be created for the sake of itself.

When the role of art evolved in this way, it exploded like fireworks above our once cherished ideals, giving way to a horde of explorations in aesthetic points of view. And so were born the eras of Aestheticism, Impressionism, Expressionism, and a whole host of other art movements that seemed to simultaneously shepherd and document the increasingly rapid changes in modern societies.

Given that a lot has happened since that turning point until now, I wonder: how have art's assignments further evolved? Is there a consistent statement we can make about art for the current ethos, or have we all gone our separate ways?

Art's Current Ethos

It's clear that art always appears as a reflection of its culture and time. With this in mind, the arts are wholly different than they were a hundred years ago, or even thirty years ago. We, who have for so long taken a Sunday drive to a modern museum or gallery, to look at strange objects by placard-dotted walls in cold-white rooms, can no longer do so with any fantasy about a cohesive purpose of art. Especially since the dawn of the tech revolution and the so-called death of postmodernism, we can no longer lean on a unified cultural perception, frankly, because there is none; the 'high cultures' that used to patronize and temper the creation of art have long ago given way to capitalist art critics, the opinions of celebrities, and the whims of television and movie moguls. And so, the former idea that art will become a mere commodity has become reality.

As a contemporary, free-enterprise North American, I now have the baffling choice of no less than 50 different breakfast cereals in any given supermarket. Similarly, the list of art genres we now have to choose from is like looking at the menu in a Chinese restaurant – seemingly without end.

As for the genre of so-called 'high art,' itself being subject to so many variations, you could argue its evolution in any direction: yes, high art has lost its basis in wider, more meaningful cultural and spiritual pursuits; and yes, high art has survived the storms of the last century completely intact, going to places we never dreamed it would go, asking questions we never thought it would ask.

Freedom and Responsibility

What I want to emphasize is this: art's purposes throughout the ages have radically changed, because we have changed. Though some of us still search for collective answers to the woes of humanity, we have on the whole become a smaller planet of individuals seeking more individual answers to individual problems. The viral capitalist meme has transformed many into comfort seekers, and others into spiritual seekers. But the fact is that we in the West have become seekers of our own redemption, and contractors of our own identity.

In the late 20th century postmodern world, it seemed that art had opened up to an entirely new paradigm – one that followed our own existentialist, individualist interpretations of life and cultural influence. And now, at this blurry and fragmented stage in our collective evolution, it seems the assignment of art has been given almost entirely to the artists. It appears we no longer have to bow down to the tired systems of gallery curators, publishers and theater directors. We are expected to create whatever we want, however we want, for whatever reason. The paradigm of our new creative process seems somehow without limit – and without any construct to hold onto.

This great new freedom we have been given as the pioneers of culture comes with an even greater responsibility. It is that we must now decide what it is that we're doing, and why we are doing it. As contemporary art makers, we cannot take our world-views for granted, blindly following the conventions of the corporate culture, or the political or religious ideals and doctrines we've been handed. We must navigate by the beacons of our own inimitable truths, knowing that we will inevitably collide with more status quo points of view.

We artists cannot rely on our confused, fractured cultures for a cohesive model of reality — to decide what is important or to determine how we need to shape our world. We know we cannot let our lives be controlled by governments, bankers, tech industries, and media giants. We artists know in the depths of our souls that we must choose between furthering the themes of a valueless materialism or following the spirit on a higher path.

We artists know that we are not only the reflectors of our world, we are the creators of it. Therefore, we alone are responsible for our futures, and for the visions we impress upon others that help mold their own futures.

We hold a power yet unknown to us. And we've been given a role we may not be ready for. As the late author and social critic James Baldwin once said, "The role of the artist is exactly the same as the role of the lover. If I love you, I have to make you conscious of the things you don't see."

I think Baldwin might have agreed that we have had that role for a long time. And now, in the age of the tech revolution, a widespread attention-deficit problem, and the visible destruction of our planet, I believe it's even more necessary for us to own up to it.

CHAPTER
Six

All About Creative Flow

The river is everywhere.

— Herman Hesse, Siddhartha

When Buddhist master and multimedia artist, Chögyam Trungpa Rinpoche, said, 'Art, genuine Art, is the activity of non-aggression,' I'm pretty sure he wasn't saying we shouldn't be like Charles Bukowski – going to bars, sucking down pints, getting into fist fights, and then writing novels about it. What he meant was that we, the monkey-minded humans, have a tendency to want to try to direct and control everything, even and especially unconsciously. As the thinking, ego-driven mind is compelled to know everything, and to know that it knows everything, it exhibits a kind of aggressive arrogance – because knowing is not really its job. When it tries to label, control, and manipulate a world that is in constant flux and out of its control, the result is, always, struggle.

So in making genuine art, we have to stop micromanaging. When we relax and let go of the rock in the river, we are no longer in opposition to the current of reality. We have made ourselves available to a state of being that is in synchronicity with the movement of the world. Having resigned ourselves to this Flow, our creative process then becomes virtually effortless. And since we are no longer splashing around, struggling to stay afloat, the waters begin to clear up and we can see much more.

As we explore the egoic, thinking part of the mind, it's interesting to see how its aggression is revealed in our daily lives. For instance, as we work behind our computer screens all day and obsess over our elaborate communication devices, we get caught up in our addictions to fulfilling tasks and to being in the mental space. We become so reliant on our cognitive functions that we tend to neglect the importance of the body. As a result, we become intellectually smart, and spiritually numb. We become physically disconnected from each other, from the powers of nature, and from our higher selves.

Joseph Campbell, the popular American mythologist, once talked about the Star Wars myth in much the same way:

> "See this thing up here? [pointing to his head] This consciousness thinks it's running the shop. It's a secondary organ. It's a secondary organ of a total human being and it must not put itself in control. It must submit and serve the humanity of the body. When it does put itself in control, you get this father [Darth Vader] or the man who's going over to the

intellectual side." (interview with Bill Moyers, "Joseph Campbell and the Power of Myth")

The upside is that this imbalance seems to have triggered a global response consisting of the integration of many ancient spiritual traditions, both Eastern and Western. Yet it appears many of us have yet to really tap into the core of these teachings, possibly because our western culture is still working from the rational worldview – believing that the thinking mind can figure it all out. After nearly two decades of practicing meditation, it's clear to me that we cannot think ourselves into enlightenment. I don't know of anyone who has. I also believe, you cannot think yourself into making great art.

The Felt Sense

Imagine for a moment, all of the tubes inside your body – the hundreds of miles of arteries, veins and capillaries; esophageal, ventricular, digestive, lymphatic, eustachian, and alimentary canals, vessels, and conduits that carry energy and fluids from one place to the next. The human body is a city of tunnels and highways that work in such a complex, efficient way, that even contemporary scientists are still in the dark about how much of it functions.

It's fascinating to see that, when we become conscious of the body's instinctual knowledge of the movement of energy, we tend to flow along with it. This has profound effects on our ability to access our creative Flow, as well as being a wellspring of inspiration. What happens is that, as we increase our awareness of energies through any of the five senses – seeing, hearing, smelling, tasting, and touching – the thinking mind slows down, and we have room to focus more of our attention perceptually, rather than through concepts or thought patterns.

Once we learn to adjust to our 'felt sense' mode, as Chögyam Trungpa commonly referred to it – we begin to see quite differently. Our perceptive abilities grow. Worlds open up within worlds, and we can explore the depths of our perception like deep sea divers. We start to notice that things aren't as we originally thought – the bottom of the ocean appears to be much richer, more intricate than we ever imagined.

Beingness and Wholeness

When you stop clinging to change, then everything is quite different. It becomes amazing! Not only do all your senses become more wide awake, not only do you feel almost as if you are walking on air, but you see, finally, that there is no duality, no difference between the ordinary world, and the Nirvana world.

— Alan Watts

It's interesting that when we drop into our Flow, we work from a unique kind of consciousness – one that is very much not based on our habitual, dualistic worldview. In effect, when we are in our Flow, the mind has to an extent merged with the objects it previously perceived as being separate from it. This dis-identification with the subject/object distinction pulls us into a totally different space – a place of wholeness – one that is plugged into our Source, our Higher Being. It is sometimes called 'beingness' because we are not so much doing anything, we are just feeling and being. We are no longer threatened by the existence of an 'other,' because the 'I' – what we normally perceive as ourselves – has merged with the object. The little 'me' that existed separately from the rest of the world, has become inseparable from the larger world, like a hand on a body. The hand will never feel like it's in danger from the rest of the body – we'll never go and just smash our hand with a baseball bat because we didn't like the way it was behaving. It's an inextricable part of our body.

It's the same when we are in the Flow – we have this inherent understanding that there is no danger from something 'separate,' and so everything becomes unimaginably easy. Everything just...flows.

CHAPTER
Seven

Mastering Your Flow

Your flow is as tangible and real as any locomotive, and just as powerful.

— Robert Genn

If you are not already a champ at getting into your Flow, I recommend a couple of ways you can practice it, based on my experience with it. By far the easiest way to get into to Flow, for me, has been through awareness of the body.

Normally, when we want to know something or explore the phenomenal world in some way, we look in order to see. We look for, or at, a thing, then we figure out what it is and say, "Oh, I see it, I get it!" We do this with intellectual pursuits, also. We figure out how something works by putting the smaller pieces together, until we 'see' the bigger picture of what it's all about. This is the accepted way we humans currently perceive the world, and it's the basis of the scientific method – by analyzing data, we subsequently draw a conclusion. And from that conclusion we form our bigger theories of how something works.

But there is another process of perceiving that is much more conducive to our state of Flow – and which has an instant calming effect on our constantly commentating minds. This way involves first 'seeing' the bigger picture, by becoming fully present with the body, and then looking at the details of what we're seeing. Once we're really in the body, we can perceive the miracle of life from a state of complete openness and oneness, and then we can look at the miraculous details of what is happening from that state. This is a practice I learned originally from my teachers at Shambhala Art International, and is based on Chögyam Trungpa's teachings. It has a powerful effect on the mind and doesn't take long to develop.

The Practice of Seeing and Looking

- Stand up straight, or sit up with your back straight, and close your eyes for a couple of minutes. Feel the different parts of your body, and then feel your whole body all at once.

- Then, as you open your eyes, stay connected to the body – don't switch your attention to the thoughts, just stay with your felt senses engaged. Feel everything at once, 360 degrees around your body. Let your awareness permeate your surroundings, as if you are not separate from them. Sense the completeness, the wholeness of everything. This is what we call 'seeing.'

• Once you get this part down, begin to look around while staying connected in this way. Look at the details of the whole scene. Begin to examine its parts. At this point, if you are really connected with the body, you should have the sense that there is nothing to get or to desire, because your surroundings are now, in essence, a part of your being. You're just awake, looking at the intricacies of the elements of you. You are not trying to figure anything out because what you normally call 'you,' has merged with each thing you are looking at.

If you master this technique, getting into the Flow state will become very natural. You will be able to do it wherever you are, in any situation. You'll be able to do it while standing in line at the grocery store, or sitting in your car in heavy traffic. And it will change your whole experience.

Every artist knows that she or he can see in two different ways. The ordinary way is characterized by the fact that perception is always related to accomplishing some end other than the perception itself. It is treated as a means rather than something in itself. But we can also look at things and enjoy their presence aesthetically.

— Herbert Guenther

Another very effective way to get into Flow is to master your medium. As a painter, for many years I never knew what Flow was – I had never even heard of it. I just thought you wrestled with the paint for a long time, in a school or by yourself, and then one day it just got a lot easier and you could do much more with it, because of what you learned with your hand-eye coordination. But my success as a visual artist wasn't just about hand-eye coordination, or that I had learned styles and techniques from masters. What ultimately gave me the satisfaction of creating art was being able to go beyond technique. I had learned my medium so well I no longer had to think about it. This allowed me to move my process into uncharted territory. When you see an improv jazz or rock musician going off the map, like they have entered another world – they can do that because they have mastered their instrument to a point where they could do it standing on their head. The thinking mind goes into auto-pilot, and so the focus can completely go to another place. Often the 'doer' of the act of playing the instrument ceases to be, and there is only the 'doing,' which in essence is just 'being.' This state of being is where the real magic happens. It pushes open the floodgates of inspiration, expanding our creative potential beyond what we were previously able to imagine. It does this simply because the thinking mind is no longer there to place any limitations on our experience.

Do the Work or Heal Yourself — a Catch 22

Of course there are such rare people who are able to, in a very focused, undistracted way, do their work for the sake of doing their work. But, for many years, that was not me, nor most people I have met. The majority of us, it seems, have a lot of ground to cover in the areas of self discipline and self knowledge. We are holding onto our emotional luggage so tightly that getting into Flow, at times, doesn't even seem to be an option.

Along these lines, I hear a lot of people talking about how we need to try to heal ourselves before we can commit to doing our work. In a sense, this is true, you gotta have the love to spread the love. But I've spent many years thinking I wasn't good enough, obsessively trying to fix whatever was "wrong" with me, that was keeping me from doing my creative work. In retrospect, I was living a catch-22. What I most needed to fix was just being able to settle down and do the work. When I was able to just show up and participate, getting into Flow wasn't much of a problem. I'm not sure if it's because of all the meditation I had done, or that I had just decided to do it. What I'm trying to say is, it's not necessary to spend 20 years of your life trying to fix yourself so you can do what you do and be really good at it. You can just show up and do the work, however bad it seems, however uncomfortable it may be. You might need a little guidance at first, and you may need to acquire some necessary skills. But when you can fully commit to your process the Flow will come naturally. You'll wake up one day and go, 'Oh, I'm actually really good at what I do!'

So, there's more than one way to think about Flow, and more

than one way to get into it. And we sometimes need different approaches at different times in our lives. My biggest priority is for you to have the knowledge that you can do things another way than you have before; that you don't have to stay stuck in your current blocks. When we are gentle with ourselves, when we trust our intuition and follow our resonance, getting into Flow becomes relatively easy. With a little time and persistence it will become second nature.

CHAPTER
Eight

Meditation and the Creative Process

*If the doors of perception were cleansed everything would appear
to man as it is: infinite. For man has closed himself up, til he sees all
things thro' narrow chinks of his cavern.*

— William Blake

Dear Artist,

I'm not going to coddle you and tell you that you don't have
to do deep work to be a professional artist, that you never
have to open your attic of skeletons or unleash any emotional
pit bulls. What I will say, unequivocally, is that you can make
your creative evolution a lot less difficult by adopting a few
simple practices. The truth is, because of the sheer amount of
distractions, chaos, and information that now seem to be an

obligatory part of 21st century living, we have to take counter measures. But just avoiding the chaos of life is probably not enough, and may not be the healthiest solution to the problem. A better solution might be to start with yourself.

In essence, what I have to say about that is this: there is nothing so unmanageable and so problematic as having an untrained mind. It gets you into so much trouble and into so many insufferable situations. I think it goes without saying – if you have a scattered mind, you will lead a scattered life, and a trail of disharmony and disenchantment is likely to follow you wherever you go. With a lack of focus you cannot direct your attention or hold onto healthy thoughts. You will always be jumping back and forth from one thing to another, without going deeper into your truth.

At the same time, there is nothing so enjoyable and so seemingly effortless as having a well-trained mind. When we take the time to clean up our thoughts and emotions, and to explore the nature of the mind in a focused way, we can really get a taste for what we're capable of. The experience of having freedom from our thoughts – our constant mental dialogue – is unimaginably pleasurable, and its path is inexhaustible. But we can only see this when we experience it for ourselves. Clarity of mind cannot be understood by minds that haven't tasted that clarity for themselves. This is why you cannot really convince anyone that they need to meditate. We have to figure that out for ourselves, and only when we're ready to figure it out – maybe when we get frustrated enough and have nowhere else to turn.

A Meditative Lifestyle

Meditation – in the general sense of the word, which means some kind of focused concentration and/or awareness practice – is, for me, one of those essential practices in life, like learning to read or riding a bike. As an artist, having a regular sitting meditation practice put rocket boosters on my creative process. It helped me get into Flow deeper than I was able to before, and I got better results in my work. Having a daily practice also helped me with:

• Dealing with the rest of my life more easily, so I could use my time much better and not get distracted from doing my work.

• Getting through a lot of the blocks I had, including the ability to sit down and do my work.

• Working with unfamiliar types of media, and being able to find ways to get into my process even though I didn't have a full grasp of a medium.

• Staying emotionally balanced and being able to better direct all the intense energies in my body that the creative process brought up for me.

• Letting go of result-oriented thinking and staying with the process of creation. It helped me give up caring about other people's opinions of my work.

- Making my process way more fun.

- Seeing things in a different way than before – experiencing a richer, fuller, and freer way of being. It helped me become a happier person.

It's important to know that a meditative lifestyle does not exclude or somehow dampen passion or creative initiative. A regular, focused-awareness practice will allow you to be as expressive as you like, without getting derailed by your emotions or negative thought patterns. With it, you can give yourself a quiet haven to rest and recuperate from the distractions and business of life. You can more easily tap into your internal resources and restock your creative "trout pond," as Julia Cameron, author of *The Artist's Way*, aptly calls it.

As we know, this is not a new concept – though the creative process is a meditation in and of itself, many artists throughout history have also adopted sitting meditation or other contemplative practices. Currently, there is a long list of celebrity artists – visual artists, musicians, actors, directors, and writers – who rely on, or once relied on, a daily sitting meditation practice: Adam Yauch, Marina Abramovic, David Lynch, Moby, Leonard Cohen, Jack Kerouac, Madonna, Hugh Jackman, Amy Schumer, Jennifer Aniston, Clint Eastwood, Kristen Bell, Jeff Bridges, Katy Perry, Russell Brand, Eva Mendes, Jerry Seinfeld, Gwyneth Paltrow, Laura Dern, The Beatles, Yoko Ono, Donovan, Sheryl Crow, Rick Rubin, Liv Tyler, Mike Love, Jane Fonda, Martin Scorsese, Oprah Winfrey, Steve Jobs, Cameron Diaz, Heather Graham, Judie Greer, Howard Stern, Naomi Watts, Tom Hanks, Mariel

Hemingway, and many, many more.

As we develop our senses and hone our minds through meditation practice, becoming more awake to the world around us, our creative process becomes much easier and much more fun. There is more mental elbow room, and more chances the elusive and cagey muse will end up on your doorstep.

It is not necessary that you leave the house, only sit at your table and listen. Do not even listen, only wait. Do not even wait, be wholly still and alone, the world will present itself to you for its unmasking, it can do no other. In ecstasy it will writhe at your feet.

— Franz Kafka

If you have not yet had a taste for what meditation and felt-sense practices can do for your creative process, give the practices in the next chapter a try. Dive into them and give them some time to work their magic.

CHAPTER
Nine

Scuba Training for the Artist: Exploring Your Creative Depths

Awareness practice is not just sitting meditation or meditation-in-action alone. It is a unique training practice in how to behave as an inspired human being. That is what is meant by being an artist.

— Chögyam Trungpa Rinpoche, *True Perception*

'Scuba Training for the Artist' is a name I use to describe my process of using various meditative practices I've learned over the years, with the practice of using a medium. It focuses on gaining an experiential understanding of the psychology of creativity – how our mind thinks and feels. It can help us in ways that go beyond our creative abilities, but focuses primarily on how we can use the power of our felt senses to deepen our creative process. My medium of choice is usually black Sumi ink, oil crayons, or finger paints. If you don't have any of these and don't have access to them, feel free to find something suitable to substitute. If you are a writer, or a dancer, or musician, you may want to experiment with writing out the exercises, or dancing or playing them, instead of painting them.

One more thing before we get started. *Very important!* These practices are in no way a substitute for doing your own creative work, whatever that may be. In my case, this mostly involves painting. Whatever your medium is, is not important. What is important is that we do not use these practices as a distraction from doing our real work, as they are meant to be done alongside our own creative work and I would strongly encourage you to do your work right after doing them. The beautiful thing about these practices is that they will grease the wheels for you and get you into your Flow.

The practices below are in the order I believe most people need to do them. If you feel compelled to do any of them in an alternative sequence, by all means, feel free to do that. It's more important to feel good about doing them than it is to try to do them in any particular order. Also, I have found that when one of them is really working for me, I will stick with it for awhile. I tend to trust my intuition and do the practices that feel right, for however long I need to.

Practice 1– The Art of Perception

This awareness practice will connect you to your body and allow you to clearly perceive the difference between your thinking mind and your body awareness, a.k.a. 'felt sense'. It does the same thing, basically, that a body-focused sitting meditation practice will do. If you practice regularly, it will deepen and enhance your perceptive abilities, which are immensely helpful for your creative process. If you want to listen instead of read the instructions, you can get the audio here: divinecreativity.org/practice.

1 Make sure you are in a quiet place where you can sit, uninterrupted, for about 30 minutes. Get comfortable – sit in a chair, or in a meditation posture on a cushion with your back straight. It makes no difference how you sit, as long as your back is vertical and you can stay alert.

2 Relax. Close your eyes, go inside and feel your whole body for a couple minutes. Then switch your focus to your thinking mind. Just become aware of your thoughts for about a minute. Then go back to focusing on the whole body again for another minute. Notice the difference between these two modes of focus, and more importantly, notice how you have the power to change your focus to one or the other.

3 Once you have a good, experiential understanding of this difference, change your focus again to the body. Become aware of your hearing sense. With your body absolutely still, listen to all the sounds coming from inside and outside your

body. Stay with this for five minutes.

4 Change your focus now to both your smelling and tasting senses. Remain motionless as you notice all the different smells in your nose, and then go to your mouth and become aware of what it tastes like. Continue for five minutes.

5 Change your focus again to your sight sense. With your eyes still closed, notice all the little dots and patterns and movement inside your eyelids. Continue this for five minutes.

6 Change your focus once again to your sense of touch, or bodily sensation. Remain motionless as you notice all the different sensations throughout your body. You can focus on one area at a time, and then gradually pan out to feeling the entire body as one organism. Continue for five minutes.

7 Wiggle your fingers and toes, then slowly open your eyes.

8 Notice how you feel; how things have changed.

9 Repeat this process daily, or as much as you like.

The point of this practice is not only to deepen your perceptive abilities. It will also reveal how you are using your mind when you create. You'll begin to see that you have more freedom from your thoughts, and more control over the mind. When we become aware that we are using the thinking, conceptual mind, and want to switch over to the felt sense, we can do that easily, because we know we have that power. We can then focus on how we want to be, and just let the thinking, monkey mind do the grunt work for us – the hand-eye, or body-movement co-ordination and other motor skills we want it to do.

It's also interesting that, as we gain clarity through the

practice of sensory awareness, we can begin to see how the mind actually perceives the world. As a practicing Buddhist, I often studied ancient texts that were radical in their views on human psychology and perception, even by today's standards. What many schools of Buddhism have said for over two millennia is that the mind projects onto our environment, previously made assumptions, or pictures, that are stored in our mind or in the collective consciousness, like a file system. When we look at a tree, for instance, the mind finds an existing picture suitable for the information it perceives, and then projects that picture onto the information. So, from a certain point of view, what we are looking at most of the time is habituated mental pictures.

The more we gain introspective awareness – through breath or body meditation methods, or other focused awareness practices such as this one – the more we can discover this process of perception and projection that is going on all the time. When we can actually see how we're perceiving something, the mind stops its incessant clinging, because it realizes what it was clinging to was just a picture, a concept that is not really true to our present experience.

Due to its apparent innumerable benefits, it is well worth the time and effort to develop your sensory awareness. As for our purposes here, it will help you stay centered and grounded in your daily life, and will give you the freedom to steer your creative process in whichever direction you desire.

Creation begins with a vision... All that we see, in our daily lives, is more or less deformed by our acquired habits. The artist must see everything as if for the first time: he must look at all of life like a child.

— Henri Matisse

Practice 2 – Releasing Resistance and Blocks

Often, the inner turmoil of preparing to free fall becomes unbearable. We go back and forth between to do or not to do, following our procrastination demons down endless hallways that lead us safely nowhere. Like this: when you have just sat down to start your creative practice and you remember, 'Oh – I forgot to do the dishes!' or, 'Oh – I forgot to milk the goats,' or, 'There's a dark spot on the wall... I think I should probably paint that wall, and perhaps the entire room, because it hasn't had a coat of paint in two years and doesn't have that clean, just-painted look that I like so well, which will make me feel better, so then I'll be able to do my work even better knowing my environment is more conducive to creative energies. And since I'm painting the room, I may as well paint the whole apartment, because I'm sure it needs it and it's easier just to do it all at once anyway, and while I'm on the subject, I forgot to pay the rent...' And on and on it goes. Your monkey mind is telling you that you can do your creative work another time, that there are more important things to do, even though you specifically set up this time to do that work. But your monkey mind obviously did not get the memo: Barring an absolute emergency, there is nothing more important than doing your work at the time you gave yourself to do it.

This practice will allow you to confront and release your resistance to creating. (Note: I encourage you to experiment in using your preferred creative medium with this exercise if that feels better – writing, dance, music, etc.) If you want to listen instead of read the instructions, you can get the audio here: divinecreativity.org/practice.

1 Get about ten sheets of large, newsprint paper – roughly18x24 inches. If you have some old newspapers, that will work, too. Get some crayons – I prefer a small set of oil crayons – they don't cost too much and you can get them at most craft or art supply stores, or online.

2 Get everything the way you need it to be, so you can work, uninterrupted, for about 30 minutes. I usually do this on a desk or table, sitting in a chair, but you could do it standing up and working off an easel or on the wall, or the floor – whatever works best for you.

3 Think about something related to your creative goals that you have resistance to. Relax. Close your eyes and go inside, feel your whole body, and locate and feel the resistance you have in there. Ask yourself, 'What does it feel like? What are its characteristics? Is it tense, or relaxed? What texture is it? What temperature? Is it moving or still? Expanding or contracting? Does it have a color or a form?' Get to know your resistance in this way for a few minutes, and just be there with it, without judging.

4 With your eyes still closed, ask your resistance if it wants to come up, to express itself onto the paper. If it does (it almost always does), just let it come up and go through your arm and hand and drawing tool (crayon in this case), and let it scribble however it wants to, onto the page.

5 Continue letting your resistance express itself for five minutes without stopping (set a timer if necessary).

6 Relax. Close your eyes and check in with your body. How does it feel? Is there still some resistance there? If so, repeat the exercise until you feel the resistance has completely left your body. When it's all gone (for now—it may come back, in which case you can repeat this exercise if/when it does), congratulate yourself for being amazing. Now is a great time to go do your own creative work.

The point of this exercise is to get you to see that your resistance to doing your work really does not hold power over you. You can look at it and just notice what it is, being an observer, instead of a victim of it. When you see what it really is, which is just a fear of something, most likely something unconscious like fear of success or failure, it loses its grip on you. And then you can let it come up instead of ignoring it, or worse, try to make it go away and suppress it even further. What's great about this is that you are doing real alchemy. You're directly transforming your resistance into Flow, and also into something tangible that you can easily observe and even appreciate, because those lines are, ¡hermosa, increíble! (Maybe they're not that increíble, but still...)

Practice 3 – Exorcising Fe

Continuing our fascination with aquatic metaphors – picture yourself having jumped from a small boat into the middle of the ocean. You can't see more than a few feet down, and you don't know how deep it is. You are able to swim, but you freeze up because you don't know what is beneath you – your mind brings up images of a man-eating, giant squid you once saw in a children's book, or killer whales you saw at a sea park, or massive, gnarly sharks you saw in Jaws, long ago.

The fear that comes up exists because you have dropped into the unknown. And the ego structure hates the unknown, because its function is to think that it knows. With no way of knowing, it goes into panic mode, because its existence is pulled into question.

Fear is the thing that underlies every form of procrastination and every instance of resistance you have to doing your work. Confronting our fears gives us courage, and a knowledge that we don't have to let them control us when they come up. When you shine a light on them, exposing the thoughts behind them, they tend to dissipate. And if the same fears come up again you'll have the tools to work with them.

This practice will allow you to observe and let go of deeply hidden fears you have that are blocking your creative work. (Note: I encourage you to experiment in using your preferred creative

n with this exercise if that feels better – writing, dance,
...ic, etc.) If you want to listen instead of read the instructions,
you can get the audio here: divinecreativity.org/practice.

1 Set yourself up like before – get about ten sheets of large newsprint paper, 18x24 inches or so. If you have some old newspapers those will work also. Get some crayons – I prefer a small set of oil crayons that you can get at most craft or art supply stores or online.

2 Get everything the way you need it to be so you can work, uninterrupted, for about 30 minutes. I usually do this on a desk or table, sitting in a chair, but you could do it standing up and working off an easel or on the wall, or the floor – whatever works best for you.

3 Relax. Close your eyes and go inside, feel your whole body for a minute or two, and then have the intention of letting any fears come up. Fear can manifest in different ways – as sensations, or emotions, or thoughts. What we are concerned with here is the sensations, what the fears feel like in the body. Ask the question, 'What am I afraid of?' The fear or fears will then come up and you should be able to feel them as a tightness, or movement, or heat, or something that feels a little like it doesn't belong there.

4 Once you feel the sensation of the fear, ask yourself, 'What is the thought behind this fear?' You might instantly have a thought come up that is related to the fear. Take a mental note of whatever thoughts come to mind and write them down after the exercise is over: 'I am afraid of...'

5 Now go back to bodily, felt sensation of the fear. Without judging it in any way, just observe it for a couple of minutes. Then after a while, ask it if it wants to express itself. If it

does, just let it come up and go through your arm, and hand, and crayon, and express itself onto the page, as scribbles, or however it wants to. Let it do this for five minutes or so.

6 Repeat steps 3-5 for 15 minutes, or until you no longer feel any fears when you ask the question, 'What am I afraid of?' If it's still there, keep repeating the exercise for another 15 minutes. Then, whether or not it's completely gone, congratulate yourself for doing this deep work. You may now want to go and do your personal creative work.

The point of this practice is to allow you to observe your fears, see directly what they are, and let them come up and out through the creative process. You actually use the fears to create, instead of letting them prevent you from creating. If you write them down afterwards, it will help you see which thoughts are generating certain fears. This is helpful because then you can consider changing the thoughts around a circumstance or goal to something more positive and constructive (see chapter 12 for more on changing thoughts and beliefs around your circumstances).

This exercise is good to do on a regular basis because a lot of the fear we have tends to run very deep in the unconscious mind. Addressing them consciously and consistently will really help clear them up and get you moving in the direction you want to go. You'll be able to work with much less effort because you're not spending your energy fighting with them.

Practice 4 – The Line of Compassion

If you want others to be happy, practice compassion. If you want to be happy, practice compassion.

— The Dalai Lama

Compassion is one of the things that can really motivate us in our work. Not only does it speed things up and get us synced with our purpose, it's a kind of hack to getting deeper into our process. If we're working with others in mind, inspiration will come more readily, and at a faster pace. It just amps everything up, and makes it more fun and more doable. I believe the reason it works so well is that it addresses a core reason around why we create in the first place.

As creating art sometimes needs to be a solitary act, we can grow out of touch with people. Working with compassion and love in our process connects us to a greater purpose. It keeps us in an expanded mode of being so we don't fall into isolation, or into the trap of thinking that we are better than others, or that it's 'all about me' (the little 'me' / ego). I have noticed that so many of my artist friends, including myself, have fallen into this trap. It's what leads to social awkwardness and anxiety, depression, and in severe cases, suicide. Being disconnected like this is no ride in the park, as I'm sure you know if you've ever done your work in solitude for extended periods of time.

This is a practice I learned originally from my Zen calligraphy Sensei, Yuko Halada, in Phoenix, Arizona. It will tap into your innate capacity for compassion, and give your creative batteries more energy. (Note: I encourage you to experiment in using your preferred creative medium with this exercise if that feels better – writing, dance, music, etc.) If you want to listen instead of read the instructions, you can get the audio here: divinecreativity.org/practice.

1 As in the previous practices, get about ten sheets of large newsprint paper, about 18x24 inches. If you have some old newspapers, those will work, too. Get some black ink or paint – it could even be cheap poster paint – I usually use Japanese Sumi ink, but anything black and paint-like should do. Also, you will need a paint brush. I usually use a Sumi brush, but any kind of large paint brush will work just fine.

2 Get everything the way you need it to be, so you can work, uninterrupted, for about 30 minutes. I usually do this on a desk or table sitting in a chair, but you could do it standing up and working off an easel or on the wall or floor if that feels better.

3 Relax. Take a deep breath, and let all the tension in your body release.

4 Close your eyes and bring to your imagination someone you don't know very well, perhaps someone you once saw on the street who was suffering in some way, or an animal you perceived to be in great pain. Now visualize yourself in a scene with them, sitting beside them as they are suffering. Bring up a strong feeling in your body of wanting to take the pain they are experiencing away from them. Do this for a couple of minutes while continuing your visualization of the scene. It is important that you really feel the positive

sensations that come from your compassionate thoughts. Don't think about it too much, just remember that we are working with emotions and energies in the body.

5 Now drop your visualization for this part. You are going to fill the paper with vertical lines, starting from the top left, going down to the bottom and then starting again just next to the previous line, until the whole page is filled with vertical lines from top to bottom. Now pick up your brush and dip it in some ink or paint, and take a deep breath. At the top of the breath, place the brush on the paper, and start to move it downward on the paper, very slowly, while breathing out slowly. When you run out of breath, stop the movement of the brush, take another deep breath, and as you start breathing out again, start to move the brush again – the brush only moves with the out-breath, stopping (no matter where it is on the line) with the in-breath.

6 After you do this a few times and really get the hang of it so you don't have to think about it anymore, bring up your compassion scene again and continue that process in your imagination, as you are painting the ink lines on the paper. Over time, your mind and body will sync up, your heart will open, and all of that compassion will manifest in the lines on the paper. If all of this is confusing, I understand – it's a lot to do all at once. But with a little practice you will get it, and it will feel great.

7 Continue the exercise for as long as it feels good. If it doesn't feel good, stop and do another exercise. You only want to do this one if you're able to feel the energies of compassion, and express them through the lines.

8 When you fill up the page, take a look at all of those lines. What do they feel like?

What I have noticed with this practice is that it's a lot easier to feel and express your positive energies within the confined, limited movement of the straight, vertical lines, than it is to do it without. This is because, with limited movement, we're able to forget about the physical process and go more deeply into the imagination and emotional energies. And when we sync up the process to the expression of the out-breath, our energy will flow easier. The whole idea here is to connect to your heart, then let it express itself. As we do this, we clear out a lot of stuck energies, and are thus able to feel more of what's there.

Not only that, what happens on the paper is that you now have a physical manifestation of those energies. If someone looks at those lines – if they are energetically, vibrationally, able to go there – they will feel the energies in themselves. In other words, the product of our exercise becomes a vibrational portal for others to go into and feel that sense of harmony and opening of the heart that you felt while doing them.

When I walk into a room of Mark Rothko's paintings, I immediately have a strong, positive, bodily reaction. I often wonder how this happens, and my sense is that what is on those canvases is Rothko's own emotional energies, transferred into a physical form that is both relatable and transferable. To me, that is pure alchemy. That we are able to affect other people, possibly change the course of their lives, by putting paint on a canvas and hanging it on a wall for them to look at, is one of the miracles of creation that makes art worth doing, if for no other reason.

Practice 5 – The Line of Gratitude

The essence of all beautiful art, all great art, is gratitude.

— Friedrich Nietzsche

As with compassion, gratitude is one of those heart abodes that we can be transported to spontaneously, as well as by invoking. Gratitude brings us great benefits. It calms the mind and puts us in a place that is centered and relaxed, feeling abundant and giving us life-affirming thoughts. As for the creative process, it will often work miracles, giving us more energy and enthusiasm than we knew possible.

This practice will get us into that feeling space that is so beneficial on many levels – for our process and for the rest of our lives. (Note: I encourage you to experiment in using your preferred creative medium with this practice if that feels better – writing, dance, music, etc.) If you want to listen instead of read the instructions, you can get the audio here: divinecreativity.org/practice.

1 This step is the same as in the previous practice. Get about ten sheets of large newsprint paper, about 18x24 inches. If you have some old newspapers, those will work, too. Get some black ink or paint – it could even be cheap poster paint – I usually use Japanese Sumi ink, but anything black and paint-

like should do. Also, you will need a paint brush. I usually use a Sumi brush, but any kind of large paint brush will work just fine.

2 Get everything the way you need it to be, so you can work, uninterrupted, for about 30 minutes. I usually do this on a desk or table sitting in a chair, but you could do it standing up and working off an easel or on the wall or floor if that feels better.

3 Relax. Take a deep breath, and let all the tension in your body release.

4 Close your eyes and bring to your imagination someone that you love – a family member or close friend, or someone who was close to you who passed on. Bring up a strong feeling of gratitude for some thing or things they've done for you or given you. Make it real, and feel the gratitude and love your image brings up in your body until it feels really good.

5 As with the previous exercise, you are going to fill the paper with vertical lines, starting from the top left, going down to the bottom and then starting again just next to the previous line, until the whole page is filled with vertical lines from top to bottom. Now pick up your brush and dip it in some ink or paint, and take a deep breath. At the top of the breath, place the brush on the paper, and start to move it downward on the paper, very slowly, while breathing out slowly. When you run out of breath, stop the movement of the brush, take another deep breath, and as you start breathing out again, start to move the brush again – the brush only moves with the out-breath, stopping (no matter where it is on the line) with the in-breath.

6 After you do this a couple of times and really get the hang of it so you don't have to think about it anymore, bring up

your gratitude image again and continue that process in your imagination, as you are painting the ink lines on the paper. Over time, your mind and body will sync up, your heart will open, and all of that gratitude will manifest in the lines on the paper. Give yourself some time to adjust to visualizing while using the brush and breathing. It's a lot to do at first but will become much easier with time.

7 Continue the exercise for as long as it feels good. If it doesn't feel good, stop and do another exercise. You only want to do this one if you're able to feel the energies of gratitude and express them through the lines.

8 When you fill up the page, look at your lines. What do they feel like ?

Like in the previous practice with the Lines of Compassion, you might notice here that it's much easier to feel and express your positive energies when you're limited to the movement of the straight, vertical lines as opposed to doing them in a more freeform way. And if you feel the need, you can practice doing the lines with the breath for a whole session or more before adding the visualization, to make sure you are able to coordinate the brushwork with feeling gratitude.

This practice is a good way to lighten things up if it feels like you're fighting with your medium or with your circumstances. It can radically shift your mood and is useful for almost any situation where you want to calm your mind.

Practice 6 – The Line of Intuition

The truth of the thing is not the think of it but the feel of it.

— Stanley Kubrick

Intuition is essential to doing any creative work. To make genuine art means that we let our intuition guide us. What we're mainly concerned with in accessing our intuition is bodily awareness. Like when we do Vipassana or other similar types of sitting meditation, the focus is on our physicality. We keep our attention single-pointedly there, and let thoughts come and go – just noticing them, without trying to manhandle them or make them go away.

Keep in mind, it is perfectly fine and to be expected that your thoughts will come up. The practice is just to notice that they are there – like clouds floating by in the blue sky, you can just appreciate them, then go back to what you were focusing on before – the body.

This practice will quickly give you access to your intuitive, greater Self. (Note: I encourage you to experiment in using your preferred creative medium with this exercise if that feels better – writing, dance, music, etc.) If you want to listen instead of read the instructions, you can get the audio here: divinecreativity.org/practice.

1 Get about ten sheets of large newsprint paper, roughly18x24 inches. If you have some old newspapers, they will work as well. Get some finger paint, non-toxic poster paint, or tempera paint, and put it into a bowl (large enough so you can access it easily). Make sure it's safe to get on your hands. Also, put something like a drop cloth underneath the paper you are using, so you don't end up painting the room...

2 Get everything the way you need it to be, so you can work, uninterrupted, for about 30 minutes. I usually do this on the floor, but you could do it sitting in a chair with a table, or standing up and working off an easel or on the wall if that feels better. (It can get messy, so the floor is probably your best option.)

3 Relax. Close your eyes, and take a deep breath. Let all the tension in your body release.

4 Let go of your thoughts for a moment and bring your awareness inside your body. Just feel around in there for a few minutes, focusing on different sections at a time for a few minutes, and then expanding that focus to the whole body at once.

5 Keeping your awareness on the body, open your eyes, dip your less dominant hand into the paint, close your eyes again and let your hand move wherever it wants to go on the paper without letting it come off the paper. Let your hand feel what is going on, and keep your focus there. Eventually, if you can, it's good to expand your awareness and feel your whole body while you are doing this. You can explore other levels of focus, but if you prefer one way over the other then just do that – whatever comes most naturally. Remember it's perfectly fine if you miss the paper, because you have something under it. Keep going for five minutes.

6 Open your eyes and look at your finger painting. Keeping your attention in the body, ask yourself, what does it feel like? And what does your body feel like?

7 Repeat steps 3 - 6 for 30 minutes. Also try doing it with both hands at once.

8 Now is a great time to transition into your own creative work.

Note: After you get the hang of this exercise, getting used to feeling with your eyes closed, try going through the entire process with your eyes open. Once you become accustomed to focusing on the body with open eyes, you will more easily be able to access your intuitive mind when you're doing your creative work, and in any other situation in your waking life.

Intuition comes easily when we are fully connected to the body with our awareness. Focusing inside our body like this has countless benefits, but the one we're mainly concerned with is the benefit of having access to our deeper sense of truth, the one that is unaffected by our circumstances. We can easily learn to go from the personal to the universal in our work, opening up to energies that lie beyond our conditioned patterns of behavior. This will give your process, and the product of that process, a sense of expansion and connectedness.

When you are really connected like this, one of the realizations you might have is that you are not really the one who is making things happen. Though, during our process we (our bodies) are in an act of creation, the 'I' (that sense of 'me'), is often no longer there. In that way, we are not performing the action. We are either lost in the action, or observing the action. This leaves the thinking mind, along with all of its baggage, totally out of the picture. We are left in a state of lightness and meditative awareness that is, at times, incredibly peaceful. This focused and equanimous quality will show up in your end result – the physical manifestation we call 'art'. And you, the 'artist,' merely allowed the manifestation of that art.

This realization, which I'm sure you've had if you've been working with a medium for a long time, will keep your head small, your being humble, and your process pure and uninhibited. At some point, it might come as a shock to the one who wants to be noticed for having done something great – your ego. It's a funny thing how, just when you think you've gone beyond all that shallowness, like a sea monster exploding from the black depths, your ego bleats, 'Hey, what about me?! I did this! I'm the one responsible for this oeuvre, this genius!'

And so it goes. Just know this – we all have, in some capacity, the five-year-old monster-genius that wants credit for everything. Just noticing its harmless existence will give you more clarity and let you move on, more seamlessly, with doing your work.

Practice 7 – The Emotional Laundry Chute

The artist is a receptacle for emotions that come from all over the place: from the sky, from the earth, from a scrap of paper, from a passing shape, from a spider's web.

— Pablo Picasso

Working with emotions can be difficult when we're doing our work. Not to mention, just having and dealing with emotions in general can be difficult, and at times unbearable. The job of artist somewhat implies that we're going to use emotions in our process, but that's not always the way it happens, depending on who you are and how you work. In any case, a better approach than being the stooge of our negative emotions is to use their power as a tool for expression, both as energy and as subject matter.

Emotion can be a perplexing subject to talk about because there are a lot of conflicting points of view on it. There doesn't seem to be any consistent definition, in either the psychological, spiritual, or medical communities I've come across. There is, strangely, little information out there with regards to exactly what emotions are, how they come about, or what purpose they serve. Yet emotions, it appears, are constantly informing our life decisions. Curious, no?

Defining Emotions

When I teach, I like to use the definition of 'emotion' as being a thought program stored in the body. It is a biochemical reaction caused by the brain as a stress mechanism, that manifests as physical sensation, usually a tension or strong feeling in the gut, chest, or throat areas. What happens many times is this: our cognitive mind, triggered by some current incident, generates a thought about the past that relates to that incident, and projects it into the future as something that it believes will be experienced again like it was in the past. The body then alerts us to this assumption by sending a stress signal.

A simple example is when you've experienced an incident in the past, such as a car wreck, and a memory of that incident gets triggered by something in the present moment, like a loud bang.

If we look at this in depth, it is easy to see that emotions which are triggered in this way are based on a falsehood. Memories of the past have no real relation to the future (to an upcoming present moment). We can also see that the past exists only as a memory of a present moment that has gone out of existence. The future, similarly, is only a projection of a thought, into a future moment of now. Both past and future, therefore, have no bearing on reality – they are merely conceptualizations, a product of our monkey minds.

Be aware that what you think, to a large extent, creates the emotions that you feel. See the link between your thinking and your emotions. Rather than being your thoughts and emotions, be the awareness behind them.

— Eckhart Tolle

Though emotions, especially the more perceptible, unpleasant ones, are often born from a misconception, they nonetheless serve us in several ways:

1. They let us know when our thoughts are in or out of alignment with our desires, with our higher selves, or with our higher purpose. 2. They let us know when our beliefs are being challenged or threatened. 3. They signal when the body is in danger – they are an alarm system for keeping the body alive.

This description is a bit of an oversimplification, as the emotional system can be very subtle in nature, and emotions can come up through many different avenues. But I find this approach to be useful for giving perspective on our more definable emotions as we work with them in the creative process.

An important and possibly obvious distinction to make about emotions is that they are separate from our internal guidance system – our intuition – and should not be regarded as a source of truth in and of themselves. You can probably remember important decisions you've made that were based on a strong emotion that, retrospectively, led you into a disastrous situation. I can remember stock market investments I made that weren't based on sound investment strategies but on my emotional attachments to the company and a naive infatuation with capital gains. After a stock tanked, I got scared and sold it, only to watch it later go up again — this time much higher than my initial investment. This kind of thing is of course not uncommon. What happens with strong emotions, I believe, is that they tend to cloud the mind, rendering us incapable of accessing our much wiser intuition.

How Emotions Differ

Another helpful distinction we can make is that the positive sensations we call joy, happiness, bliss, etc., work differently from negative or unpleasant emotions, in that they come from the opening of the heart, or from an alignment of the body, mind and spirit – what we might call love. When our hearts open up because of a reaction to a circumstance, or as the result of a thought or otherwise, we are very much in the present, feeling everything in that moment. This is usually a very positive experience – because we are accepting, not rejecting, our circumstances, and therefore have opened up to our felt senses and are no longer relying on our thinking mind. We're not obsessing about the past or the future, which so often results in negative feelings – some kind of tightness or fear associated with it. You could say that pleasant feelings or emotions are the result of an expansion, or opening, while unpleasant emotions, such as anger, pride, jealousy, etc., are born out of some kind of fear or rejection of circumstances, and are therefore contracting in nature.

As for our explorations of emotions in the creative process, whether they are positive or negative, coarse or subtle, I find it's best to observe them as they come up and to feel them directly, keeping a kind of detached awareness of them as you work. As many of us have a tendency to suppress our emotions, the practice of direct observation will help to change that habit. And remember – you have complete dominion over your emotions, and can use their power, ju-jitsu-like, for your creative process.

Rational thoughts never drive people's creativity the way

emotions do.

— Neil deGrasse Tyson

The point of this practice is to become accustomed to giving your emotions the mic. (Note: I encourage you to experiment in using your preferred creative medium with this exercise if that feels better – writing, dance, music, etc.) If you want to listen instead of read the instructions, you can get the audio here: divinecreativity.org/practice.

1 Get about ten sheets of large newsprint paper, about 18x24 inches. If you have some old newspapers those will work also. Get some finger paint, or non-toxic poster paint or tempera paint, and put it into a largish bowl so you can access it easily. Just make sure it's ok to get on your hands. Also, put something like a drop cloth or some plastic underneath the paper you are using, so you don't end up painting the room. (This exercise can also be done with a brush and ink, or a piano or ukulele, or your voice, or writing pen, etc.) I also like to use my less dominant hand for this so that there's less chance that my

cognitive mind will take over – it doesn't really know how to paint with this hand, and the less we 'know' how to do this, the better.

2 Get everything the way you need it to be, so you can work, uninterrupted, for about 30 minutes. I usually do this on the floor, but you could do it sitting in a chair with a table, or standing up and working off an easel or on the wall if that feels better. (Keep in mind it's a messy process.)

3 Relax. Take a deep breath, and let all the tension in your body release.

4 Let go of your thoughts for a moment and bring your awareness inside your body. Just feel around in there for a few minutes. Bring your awareness to an emotion that is drawing your attention. If you can't find any that's fine, just think about something that didn't go well for you in the recent past and it should appear pretty quickly.

5 Focus your awareness on the sensation of the emotion. What does it feel like? What are its characteristics? Is it hot or cold or somewhere in between? Does it have a texture or color? Does it have a shape? Is it moving or still? Stay with the sensation of it for a couple minutes.

6 Then after you have a good sense of what it feels like, ask it if it wants to express itself. I realize this is a little weird, talking to your emotion like a psyche patient, but trust me, it works.

7 If it does want to come up and express itself (it usually does, so just wait until it feels like it wants to release) open your eyes, dip one or both hands into the paint, and let the emotion(s) come up and express itself/themselves through your hands and paint, onto the paper. Do this with your eyes open for 60 seconds. Stay connected to the emotional sensations in the

body while this is happening.

8 Relax, and look at what happened on the paper. Keeping your attention in the body, ask yourself, what does it feel like? When you look at it, does it feel like the emotion you felt in your body?

9 Repeat steps 3-8 for 30 minutes.

10 Congratulate yourself. Now is a great time to transition into your own creative work.

I must admit that this is one of my favorite practices, both to teach and to do. I haven't had a student in any of my classes dislike the process. Most of them are relaxed and glowing after just 20 minutes doing it. For me it's a totally liberating experience, especially since I'm someone who had a lot of suppressed emotions in the past. Additionally, when I discovered I could directly process emotions and at the same time create great work, it was like learning real magic – emotions came up that I never knew were there, and they came out in such a beautiful and profound way, all by themselves, with little to no effort on my part.

When you get more comfortable using your emotions like this, you might come to realize that they don't hold as much power over you as they used to. This is one of the great benefits and privileges of using emotion in creative work. We get to know the nature of this beast firsthand, and why it does what it does. As this process becomes more natural for us, we develop more space around our emotions. We begin to let go of our identification with them. Eventually, we become more like the kind of person who can express their emotions gracefully, and without inhibition – and like a person who wears few emotional triggers, because they have, in essence, tamed their dragons.

CHAPTER
Ten

Discipline Invokes Genius

Genius at first is little more than a great capacity for receiving discipline.

— George Eliot

The New Oxford American Dictionary describes 'discipline' first and foremost as, 'the practice of training people to obey rules or a code of behavior, using punishment to correct disobedience: a lack of proper parental and school discipline.' This is the definition of discipline I grew up with. It's no wonder I didn't really cotton to the idea of it. Oxford's third definition seems much better – 'activity or experience that provides mental or physical training: the tariqa offered spiritual discipline | Kung fu is a discipline open to old and young.' This one works for me, but I'm still not really satisfied, so let's make our own. Discipline: commitment by an individual to an activity or experience that offers abilities or personal development. Commitment, for me, is key to the concept of discipline. And I'm not so sure we can develop this commitment without passion or some kind of strong internal motive. In my experience, you have to really want something to commit to it, to have the discipline to carry it out.

When I first started painting and drawing, I got my discipline mostly through other people. I hung around artists who inspired me until I got enough energy from them to do my own work. My discipline waxed and waned for years until I really knew what I wanted — until I understood why I was here on this planet. After that, working hard wasn't so much a problem anymore because I wanted to do it, because I saw meaning and purpose in it.

Just Do It

You can only become truly accomplished at something you love. Don't make money your goal. Instead, pursue the things you love doing, and then do them so well that people can't take their eyes off you.

— Maya Angelou

I am inclined to want to instill this idea in you, dear Artist. If there is one thing you get out of reading this book, let it be this: once you know what your true purpose in life is, just do it, and keep doing it. I'm guessing you already know what that is. If you really don't know, you might want to find a coach or mentor or someone who can help. This is the most important discovery you will have in your entire life, because once you have that, discipline becomes duck soup. You can stop putting conditions on your ability to take action, and just let go and follow your intuition. And you can quit putting up with people who try to get you to do things that aren't your things to do.

Discipline Requires Flexibility

I had a friend named Haider who I met on the street in New York when I was living in the East Village. He was a disciplined human rights journalist, working at the U.N. Due to a drinking problem, he got kicked out of his apartment, so he would sleep on the street and get up at six in the morning to continue to write and publish his human rights articles as he had done for the past 13 years. Eventually he lost his job as a reporter at the U.N.

On a good day, Haider was the kind of person you couldn't help but admire. He would talk to you in a way that was so pure and so full of love that it would light a fire in your heart. I would often hang out in the park with him and we'd talk about politics, or he would recite his Sufi-like poetry, or do a silly dance when the Chinese ladies would come out at night to do their musical aerobic routine. And he had a laugh that sounded like a truck horn in an earthquake. It was so loud and so powerful it seemed to shake the ground.

As it turned out, my friend Haider sabotaged himself through drinking and unruly behavior because he realized many people in the higher echelons of the U.N. were not really interested in human rights. From his point of view, they were giving in to greed instead of helping to improve people's lives. What I think happened on a deeper level was that he became so identified with his role as a U.N. reporter that when he saw that the organization he had given his whole life to was corrupt, it shattered him. He wasn't able to let it go.

Haider's story illustrates an important point: discipline requires flexibility. If we're too identified with our external role in life, and something changes, we can get really stuck. We have to tread lightly, not mistake the waves for the ocean, and not get attached to the form our discipline takes – to the context of our creative work.

Easier said than done. I've had friends who got stuck and either sabotaged themselves or committed suicide because they didn't get this memo. I have personally sabotaged myself many times because I did not get this memo: our commitment, in our discipline as artists, is to our process; it is not to the subject matter, medium, or product of our process. This is the one thing we can never forget. It's what makes or breaks us in the end: We, the creators, must never get attached to circumstances or to what we create, for any reason whatsoever.

The ability to differentiate between your process and its context will give you freedom and flexibility with your work. You will bounce back from any difficult circumstances when you know this, and be able to continue to stay in your flow.

You'll be a happy artist, and not go the way of those bright stars we all know who crashed or burned out because they couldn't see the bigger picture.

Creative Discipline – Making up our own Rules

One of my most cherished times as a visual artist was when I became part of a guerrilla art group in Cincinnati, Ohio. It was so satisfying because we could put our art out onto the street where it really mattered. We could reach the common person with our messages for social justice – and we didn't have to go to the trouble of organizing some kind of venue gathering. Our venue was the street, and it was always available to show our work.

In addition to making street art, I always loved walking around and looking at murals and guerrilla art in metropolitan areas because they are often done without regard to the current trends in art, or with the point of mocking those trends. There is always something so refreshing about seeing work that shamelessly ignores the fashions of art.

I remember once when I was walking around lower Manhattan, I saw a homeless guy charging tourists ten dollars to lift up his big piece of cardboard that covered a Banksy painting on the wall of a building. I wondered if Banksy was supporting homeless people with his art in this way. Whatever his actual reasons are for doing what he does, it's evident he has raised the bar to the sky for those of us who never thought we could have success while so blatantly disregarding the rules of the art game. After his latest punch in the face to the 'high art' world — by selling a self-shredding painting at Sotheby's auction — it's clear that he has become the poster child of civil disobedience and social activism in art.

I never took guerrilla art anywhere near the level that Banksy did, but personally, I have often felt that breaking rules is the most responsible thing I could do. Not because I am an anarchist, trying to save the world by driving through stop signs. Many of society's rules are not actually helpful – especially the rules surrounding the idea of how to be a successful human, which are so often based on following the perpetual carrot of economics and not on personal or spiritual development. If I have an understanding that I am the creator of my life, then I am responsible to question the rules set before me, to see whether or not they actually support my life's purpose.

This is what I call Creative Discipline. We make up our own rules as we go, because in the end, we are the creators of our lives. This is an important point because ultimately our success hinges on it: the rules we design and live by must adhere to the principles of our own divine purpose. That purpose, which is given to us through our human intuition, and through being gentle and honest with ourselves, is always in sync with the greater purpose of all other human beings and with all of nature.

When we are truly in touch with our intuition, our Creative Discipline reveals itself quite naturally, and the need to live by other people's rules falls away. We realize, for example, that we no longer have to follow some religious organization's behavioral ideals – though our own Creative Discipline will always be in line with the ethical standards of most ancient spiritual traditions – the biblical Ten Commandments, the

Buddhist Freedom Vows, the yamas and niyamas of Patanjali's eightfold yogic path, and so on – because our true purpose is fundamentally aligned to the higher laws upon which those traditions are based.

Once we have a good connection with our higher Self, also known as Source/God/Allah/Krishna/Mother Earth, Father Sky/Buddha/Tao/Brahmin, we can get into our Flow more easily and deeply. And being in Flow gives us a deeper connection to Creative Discipline, which in turn helps us establish an even more direct path to our Source. And around and around we go, into and out of the revelatory process of divine creation, the great and mysterious ocean of beatitude that lies quietly beneath the surface of our otherwise distracted, mundane human lives.

CHAPTER
Eleven

Authenticity is Freedom

Nothing is original. Steal from anywhere that resonates with inspiration or fuels your imagination. Devour old films, new films, music, books, paintings, photographs, poems, dreams, random conversations, architecture, bridges, street signs, trees, clouds, bodies of water, light and shadows. Select only things to steal from that speak directly to your soul. If you do this, your work (and theft) will be authentic. Authenticity is invaluable, originality is non-existent. And don't bother concealing your thievery – celebrate it if you feel like it. In any case, always remember what Jean-Luc Godard said: "It's not where you take things from – it's where you take them to."

— Jim Jarmusch

When I lived in the East Village of Manhattan, I would walk or bike around the neighborhood often, just to explore the area and see what was going on. One time I was walking through Astor Place and passed by a crowd of people with their phones in the air, photographing something. I inched my way through the crowd to see what the spectacle was: a very long-haired, extremely bearded and hairy Jewish-looking man, wearing a white tutu skirt and sneakers, and nothing else. He was mysteriously fondling props and shouting inanities at the audience in a very non-conceptual, Dada-like way. He was captivating. I couldn't help but watch as he danced around, shouting, "Love, love, love, love, love is all there is!" I didn't know what was going on inside me, but I felt different than before I saw him – much better somehow.

That man, I found out later, was Matthew Silver, street artist extraordinaire, who soon became a local legend. After that, I often wandered around the neighborhood looking for him on a street corner or in a neighborhood park, to see the evolution of his 'act.' Sometimes he would wear a bright green and yellow speedo with nothing else but tennis shoes, looking like the unlikely offspring of Frank Zappa and Jesus Christ. The thing I loved most about him was that he was so obviously himself. There was no pretense about his madman performance – it was just him acting out his passions, which were just to love people and get them to take off their battle armor and come join his non-sequitur, love-party fun-circus.

Magic is more real than the machine — where we're doing things that have nothing to do with love, and the soul, and the spirit.... By me doing this I'm testing the world, and I'm reminding myself and others that the magical world still exists [....] We're not overcome by the wasteland yet.

— Matthew Silver, 'Who is Matthew Silver? Legendary NYC Street Performer,' (Youtube, 2017).

Matthew's Secret

And this, as I subsequently discovered, is Matthew's secret: he loves himself and his vision so immaculately and unconditionally that he doesn't really care what other people think of him. He's so absolutely free of criticism and judgment that most people, I'm quite certain, think he's a nutball. I like to think of him as an example of what is sometimes called *theia mania* – divine madness, or crazy wisdom – which is enlightened behavior that transcends societal norms. It's not madness, but a state of spiritual ecstasy, where you are so identified with your higher Self that you go beyond the dualistic, conditioned mind to a place of complete openness and innocence. People who are in this state are often highly self-aware individuals who have no agendas other than to explore the limitations of the phenomenal world and to express the bliss of having gone beyond it. And so every known social rule tends to go out the window, and they might seem a little bit crazy to anyone who is not where they're at.

Matthew might be an extreme example of someone who is authentically himself and who is committed to his purpose in life. But to me he represents one of the hallmarks of spiritual or creative genius. He seems to have what every brilliant, creative human spark in history had, who was able to explore, without moderation or social prudence, the little known world of the larger Self – the soul of one's being which transcends societal programming because it does not see circumstances as problems, but as the miracle of life. When I saw Matthew Silver dancing around, shouting like an idiot, I could feel the soul of my being. I felt absolutely inspired, not to be like him, but just to be, however imperfectly, myself.

Be yourself – everyone else is already taken.

— Oscar Wilde

You Are the Buddha

One really interesting phenomenon that came out of going head-first into a spiritual life for me was this: when I saw my own true authenticity, I could never really give my power away again.

After being involved with so many teachers over the years, I finally came to terms with the idea that it was, in fact, their job to insult me. I realized that they were only insulting the 'me' I thought I was – the mind of thoughts and emotions that, paradoxically, thinks it has to suffer to be happy; the part of me that is conditioned to think it has to be something it's not, in order to fit into the world.

And though my teachers, to the contrary, also tried to tell me over and over again 'You are the buddha,' I didn't believe it. The power that I was trying to get from them was already inside of me, and they were merely pointing the way to it. I didn't see the simplicity of this because I was looking for something that was complex and out of reach. My mind looked for solutions outside instead of looking in at itself, because it didn't want to know the real truth – that it does not know the location of the holy grail. One of my favorite teachers, Lester Levenson, who passed on long ago, once said, "If you want complexity, you'll never see simplicity." For so long I was looking with my monkey mind for something it didn't have the depth to see.

After I had this understanding, I stopped trying so hard and started to let go into my own way of being. I discovered the value of following the resonance of my own path, which I now see has no end. I learned that the unbounded Self that is unconcerned for the fruits of its labor, that exists just to be what it is, whole and complete – that Self is true authenticity, and it is the path to freedom.

One thing I know for certain, is that once you see the depth of your ocean of authenticity, you will stop giving away your power – to gurus, to parents, to bosses, to lovers, and everyone else. You will understand the importance of your own unique contribution, and you'll stop giving all of your time to other people's projects instead of doing your own work. You will never go back to trying to fit in to other people's ideas of what your life should look like, ever again – because being your true self is the secret to your genius, and because living life on your own terms feels better than anything else.

Sure, you will still have bills to pay, and you may have to keep your day job for now. But your creative capacity will bloom like never before, and you will see opportunities everywhere you look. You will begin to see that you are not separate from your purpose, and that nothing can stop you from being and doing what you are — no matter your circumstances.

Just State the Facts

As for the practicalities of the creative life, to say that authenticity creates value is true, but maybe a bit superficial. Authenticity makes people want what you have, because what everyone really wants is self-love and self-acceptance. So when you have that thing that everyone else wants, you can shine your light through your art, out into the confused, stressed out crowds who still think they have to try to fit into a system to survive or to be happy.

And you won't have to really try so hard anymore, to make so much effort, because there's nothing outside of your own being, or your own experience, that holds such great importance. And so your job as artist becomes very simple. I remember my favorite prose poem by Leonard Cohen – How to Speak Poetry – apt advice to young poets: "Avoid the flourish," and just state the facts. I believe it was his way of saying, 'stop whining about your idealistic flotsam, and let go and let the world move through you – because you're not what you think you are – you're not the seeker of your experience, you are the director...you are the gate keeper.'

Take the word butterfly. To use this word it is not necessary to make the voice weigh less than an ounce or equip it with small dusty wings. It is not necessary to invent a sunny day or a field of daffodils. It is not necessary to be in love, or to be in love with butterflies. The word butterfly is not a real butterfly. There is the word and there is the butterfly. If you confuse these two items people have the right to laugh at you. Do not make so much of the word. Are you trying to suggest that you love butterflies more perfectly than anyone else, or really understand their nature? The word butterfly is merely data. It is not an opportunity for you to hover, soar, befriend flowers, symbolize beauty and frailty, or in any way impersonate a butterfly. Do not act out words.
Never act out words.

— Leonard Cohen, "How to Speak Poetry"

CHAPTER
Twelve

Reinventing Yourself: Changing Core Beliefs

The tribal mentality effectively indoctrinates an individual into the tribe's beliefs, ensuring that all believe the same. The structure of reality – what is and is not possible for the members of the group – is thus agreed upon and maintained by the tribe.

— Caroline Myss

Dear Artist,

Shortly after I turned 39, I decided to hitchhike across the U.S. for three weeks with no money, no food, and no destination. My plan was that I would try to let go of any ideas or beliefs about who I was in my normal life, and just be in the moment and go wherever people took me.

What happened in those three weeks remains difficult to describe. What I can say is that what started out as a strange and curiously funny adventure, turned into some kind of Gus Van Sant drifter movie escapade, becoming more surreal with each day. I eventually found myself traipsing across the continent in a Winnebago full of Grateful Deadheads, begging for gas from strangers, and sleeping in the parking lot of Walmart.

Overall, the biggest revelation I had about the experience was how remarkably kind people were. I noticed that, the more I decided to trust people, the more they wanted to help me, often going beyond my expectations of them. I met other, more experienced hitch hikers who also seemed to know this. Many of them were twenty-something kids who had no money, but had street smarts, and just wanted to get across the country. Maybe it was out of necessity, but it seemed like they had a sincere belief in the goodness of complete strangers – they just hitched around the country like it was a time-honored tradition.

It's easy to see the world from a different perspective when you're standing in the margins of the roads with your thumb in the wind. There were times when I saw the dark side of hitchhiking in America. At one point, somewhere in Oklahoma, after the 900th car passed by with no sign of stopping, I reminisced about my days of hitching rides in India – about how easy it was because people didn't hesitate to stop. For whatever reason, they were genuinely interested in giving you a ride.

In that moment, I wondered why we, the people of this vast, Western continent, with it's long, smoothly-paved highways, and perfectly square city blocks, are such a fearful bunch. It seems so many of us have become inured to violence, and accustomed to our fear of strangers. We have conditioned ourselves with movies, television, newscasters, and our myriad prescription drug addictions, to escape the pain of life by insulating ourselves from it. We have learned it's best to limit our experiences so that we can remain within the bounds of a safe, cultural normalcy – rarely venturing out to cross the borders of our comfort zones.

Tragically, this more or less applies to the art cultures as well. I have seen, and heard, so much art that is comfortably benign, that takes no cultural risk because the artist hasn't done the deep work of putting themselves on the line and discovering what they're really here for. Thankfully though, I have also been inspired to see so many artists who have done their difficult work – who persevered through the tough times and clearly have something to show for it.

Belief and Self Identity

And it suddenly dawns on you that you've arrived with a certain sense of having been cheated, because it is just the same life as it always felt. And you are conditioned to be in desperate need of a future. [...] So that one [...] is educated to live in the future and one is not ever educated to live today.

— Alan Watts

I think it's safe to say we're all programmed in our own

way – by our childhoods, by our trauma, our general life experiences, and even past life experiences. Psychologists say that our minds have indiscriminately absorbed other people's behaviors from the time we were born, up to the age of seven. According to this idea, ever since this age we've been more or less on autopilot, unknowingly defining our experiences and attracting circumstances based on these initial influences.

On top of that, we're wired to echo the people around us at any given moment, like self-herding sheep, to walk and talk and think like everyone else. This is a hard thing for some of us to admit, but I see it happening everywhere I go – and I see the tendency in myself, as well.

And so, you might wake up one day, and say, 'I don't like the life I'm living, I want to make a change – a very big change.' And that is a great and beautiful thing, just that you know that. But here's the thing: when we decide to make a major change in our lives, our conscious determination often runs contrary to the hidden, deeply ingrained habits of our unconscious mind. Like a wave trying to move the ocean, it can have few lasting effects on our experience, because the unconscious programming is so much bigger and more powerful. It's the 'man behind the curtain' – it determines not only how we react to the world, but also colors how we perceive the world in the first place, and so, it dictates much of our reality.

The difficulty lies not so much in developing new ideas as in escaping from old ones.

— John Maynard Keynes

You might have heard the story about how elephant trainers in many parts of the world domesticate elephants. The younglings are tied with a rope to a small stake, and they cannot pull out the stake because they're not big enough. When they grow to become full-sized elephants, they have the ability to uproot the stake and to escape, but they don't, because they still identify with the younger elephant's belief that the stake is too strong for them to pull out.

Maybe you've noticed – limiting beliefs are one of the most difficult things to uncover. We don't see them until they grow up from the roots and sprout like weeds in the cracks of the sidewalks. For whatever reason, we're blind to them – not to mention, we're also unaware that they're driving our experience most of the time.

When I started to uncover my own hidden, limiting beliefs, I was shocked to discover that I was like the elephant tied to the stake. My efforts to do great things with my art were tethered to a belief that I didn't deserve to be successful at it.

Argue for your limitations, and sure enough they're yours.

— Richard Bach

The Function of Limiting Beliefs

Ultimately, we are eternal, infinite beings. We have chosen, knowingly or unknowingly, to take on beliefs that limit our experiences. The function of limitations, however, is not accidental – it's what allows us to have an experience in the first place. If we did not have the very specific limitations of the human body – the five felt senses and the thinking mind – we would not be able to see a vast, bright blue sky, or the tiny articulations of a variegated, red-orange autumn leaf. We would just be a big, nebulous blob of whatever-ness, incapable of having a unique human experience.

The limitations of belief work in the same way. They shape our perception into a specific point of view, and give us the opportunity to learn and to evolve from one experience to the next.

If you think about your limiting beliefs in this way, you might not beat yourself up after realizing you took on the fundamental belief, for example, of being a person who is not able to make great art. You can just say, 'I had this belief that was serving me up until a point (because not being able to make great art does have its advantages – for instance, you'll never be a target for the negative rants of art critics, nor will you alienate those close to you who have become envious of your success), and now I want to experience something different, so I can take on a new belief that supports my new, desired experience of making great art.'

If we turn our attention inward and let the monkey mind calm down, it becomes easier to spot the programs we're running, and see which ones no longer serve us. Then we can begin to replace the old ones with shiny new ones that better reflect our desires. In this way, we can define ourselves as the artists we want to be, instead of being defined by our old programs. And from there, the process of making big changes becomes much easier – our beliefs are now aligned to our desires, so we can pull out the stake and take ourselves and our creative process in the direction that's most exciting for us.

Our ultimate act of creativity is giving birth to who we are....

— Matthew Fox

A Practice for Changing Limiting Beliefs

There are many different practices for changing your unconscious programming. Here is a method I use, which is inspired by both Bentinho Massaro's, and Teal Swan's methods of finding and changing core beliefs. It's an exercise that will shed light on the beliefs and habit patterns that are no longer serving you. It uses your intuitive powers to help you define, and adopt, new beliefs that will resonate with your higher self.

Changing Your Limiting Beliefs Practice, Part 1

• Think of something you have been struggling with in your life, such as making a series of paintings that you really like. Write down that struggle. Then, write a statement admitting defeat to your struggle. For instance, you might say, 'I can't seem to make art the way I want to make it – it never turns out as something I like, or something that I can really value.

It's obvious, I really suck at painting and I'll probably never be good at it.'

• Give in to your actual thoughts about the struggle, being honest and admitting, for instance, that you think you are incapable of realizing a goal. This will help you loosen your mental grip on the apparent belief, and give you a sense of relief, so you can move on to narrowing down which core, subconscious beliefs are supporting it.

• Then, write down the answer to the questions, 'If this is really true, why is it a struggle, and why is it such a bad thing?' Then ask the question, 'What does this mean? (to me, or about me)' Write your answers to these questions, and then ask the same questions, again, about your answer. Repeat this process until you get an answer that feels like it can't go any further, like it can no longer be answered again.

• You might immediately find the core, limiting belief around your obstacle, and that is, of course, ideal. But often, we have a complex array of thoughts surrounding an issue, with one or two very core beliefs being at the root of the problem. By writing continuously, we will get closer and closer to sussing out which ones are our base programs. Keep in mind, your core belief(s) are likely to be something completely different than what you might have imagined. For example, instead of being afraid of failure, you might fear success – or instead of the belief being about yourself, you may be compensating for someone else, feeling responsible for how they feel – and so on.

• Once you have a good idea about which thought or thoughts are your basic programs, write it/them down as a statement of belief. You can then change this limiting, core belief with a simple exercise:

Changing Your Limiting Beliefs Practice, Part 2

• Sit comfortably, with a straight spine, in a chair or on a cushion, and close your eyes. Focus your attention on your body for a minute or two, and then make your core belief statement – for example: 'I cannot make great art because I am unworthy.' Let your intuition tell you if this statement is beneficial to your goal, or not — or more aligned to your higher self, or not. (Hint: if it feels contracting or unpleasant in your body when you say it, it is not in alignment with your goal, or with your higher self.)

• Then, decide whether or not you really want to change this belief. If so, create a positive (perhaps opposite) statement that feels more aligned with your goals, such as, 'I can produce art at a level I feel good about, because I am worthy. I might need to take some painting classes, show up every day, and stay focused on my process, but I know that I can do it.' Close your eyes again, and ask yourself if this statement is true (more in alignment). If it feels really good, keep repeating the statement in your mind for a few minutes, getting used to how it resonates in your body when you say it.

• If the new thought does not feel completely right, repeat the process, with your eyes closed, of testing new thoughts which feel more aligned with your higher self and your goals. You will eventually, if not immediately, find a statement that really resonates with you, that feels really good when you say it. Voilá, you have just begun reprogramming your belief! Repeat your new positive statement with your eyes closed, for five minutes, every day, for two weeks. This will give your mind enough time to fully digest it. It's also a good idea to repeat the entire exercise on a daily basis, with the same or similar issue in mind, to make sure you find all the limiting, core beliefs associated with that issue.

To recap:

- **Part 1**

- Write down your struggle, admitting defeat to it.

- Write down the answers to the questions, 'If this is really true, why is it a struggle / why is it such a bad thing?' And then ask, 'What does this mean? (to me, or about me)' Then ask the same questions, again, about your answer. Repeat this process until you get an answer that feels like it won't go any further when you repeat the questions.

- Write your last, core statement of belief: 'I believe that....'

- **Part 2**

- Close your eyes, focus your attention on the body, and then mentally say your old, limiting, core belief statement. (Note: if saying your core belief to yourself does not feel good, it is definitely not true or beneficial, according to your intuition, or higher self.)

- Then, decide whether or not you really want to change this belief. If so, create a positive (perhaps opposite) statement – a new thought that is more in line with who you want to be. Test it with your intuition, saying it mentally, with your eyes closed. If it feels good to the body, it is true, or beneficial, according to your higher self.

- Keep thinking positive thoughts which relate to your issue, until you find the one that feels the best to you.

- Once you find a new thought/belief that really resonates with your higher self, repeat that thought like a mantra in your mind for a few minutes, feeling the resonance in your body as you say it.

- Write down that new belief as a statement: 'I believe....' Congratulate yourself for doing this deep work.

- Repeat this exercise daily for two weeks (repeating your new, positive belief, and/or the entire exercise).

The key to this exercise is knowing that our beliefs, being merely habituated, unconscious thought programs, cannot ultimately be true or false. It would be like saying the operating system on your computer is true or false. It's neither, of course – it's just the information that tells the physical hardware how to function. If the operating system is out of date, or has some kind of virus or coding bug in it, the computer doesn't work right – it becomes glitchy. It's the same for us humans – we become glitchy when our old beliefs don't serve us, or when they don't resonate with the truth of our higher selves. Once we shed light on a belief, becoming conscious that it is, in fact, an obstacle to our goals and to living out our higher purpose, it will usually lose its power over us and naturally dissolve.

At that point, in staying connected to the body and being more in tune with our intuitive mind, we can consciously implant a new belief in the mind, and then make it habitual through the process of repetition, and through finding evidence in our daily life that supports it.

Additionally, a way to ensure your new belief will stick, is to make it real for you. It's probably not a good idea to jump from, 'I suck at painting,' to 'I am the planet's most sought after visual artist.' Be gradual about it and ramp it up – be realistic about what you are able to accept at this time. Remember, many of your deeply held beliefs have been there a very long time, so uprooting and replacing them will most likely require a little time and patience.

CHAPTER

Thirteen

The Wealthy Artist

Making money is art and working is art and good business is the best art.

— Andy Warhol

Dear Artist,

I remember well the days where I didn't know where my next check would come from, or when. At one point while living in lower Manhattan, working as a handyman and starving as an artist, I went into the subway and bought a ticket to Hoboken for a potential job, with the rest of the money in my bank account. I had just enough for that one-way ticket, and not enough to get back home. Had I not gotten that crappy, underpaid freelance job that day, I wouldn't have had a way to get back home that night, or I would have had to jump the turnstiles in the subway. For some reason I just trusted that it would be ok, and somehow it worked out.

As artists, we are often regarded as people who have problems paying the rent, and our belief in this myth only adds to its truth. What I've noticed over the years working as a visual artist and a freelance designer is that whenever I let go of this myth and stopped worrying about my circumstances, things somehow always fell into place — I never went hungry and I always had a roof over my head. There is something about taking a leap and believing that the universe will support us that actually works magic.

If we take a look at wealth and money in a more conventional way, most of our questions can be answered by considering how we are creating value, and how we value ourselves, the creators — money, as it turns out, is merely a form of energy that comes to us because we have created some kind of value for others.

In looking at money as energy, you can see how it relates to the energy you put into your work. Have you ever looked at a painting, or listened to a song, and it was obvious that the artist was self-absorbed and stuck in their egos? I often see art like this in cafés, where it looks like the person is emotionally shut down, and they are trying to make something based on their concepts or interpretations of other people's art. It's shocking to me how many people still do not understand that making art is not about learning some technique.

So then, you could ask yourself, what kind of energy are you putting into your work? Does your creative process involve you actually feeling something? Is it moving you in some way emotionally, is it touching your soul? Are you open to what is coming through you in your process, letting yourself go deep into the Flow? Or are you thinking about being able to pay your bills, or about appeasing someone else's aesthetic sensibilities with your work?

Value

Our 'art' – by which I mean, the product of our process – is a blueprint of our state of mind, and of how we feel when we are creating. You really cannot fake it, because your work will hold the vibrations you put into it. Like a stock chart or a lie detector, it will always tell the truth. If your intention or state of mind is beatific and confident, it will present that. If it is dumbed down or boringly derivative, it will show that. So if we want to create some kind of beauty, to express something in our own unique way to the world, this is an important consideration – what we think and feel is valuable.

Even if your technique is not up to snuff, if your art is done with passion, it will show that passion, and it will move people in some way. I don't care what kind of art you are making – there is someone out there who will value what you do if your heart is really in it, precisely because your heart is in it. So don't think you have to master your medium before you can start earning a living with your work.

I had a friend who once made small, very primitive paintings of trees on cardboard scraps. He literally just started painting for the first time in his life – he borrowed a brush and some black ink from me, and started creating these pieces in the park. Then a month went by, and he told me he had sold many of them to his friends for $100 each. The paintings were technically horrific, but they were spirited, they had an honest eagerness about them, and they were unique. You could very clearly see in them his love of trees, and his immense admiration for the beauty of nature.

So even if you haven't been doing your work for long, when you keep showing up, committing to your process with feeling, you will inevitably move into deeper layers of your being. Your art, in turn, will show that, and become more valuable. People will see that you have gone to a place where most people don't go, and they will value that depth, that connection to something greater.

Currency

You can think of your energy – or the love you put into your work – as a type of currency. The more love you put into your process, the more currency you have in your bank. This might sound really woo woo, but hear me out. The more you let your love-energy currency flow into the world, by physically getting your art out into the world and in front of the right people, the more it will flow back to you, in whatever form of currency that is useful to you. This is natural law – the Law of Compensation – you reap what you sow, as they say. It is like a revolving door of energy, cycling back and forth, often returning to you even more than you gave in the first place.

In a nuts and bolts way of speaking, it's very simple: people give us money for our art when it moves them to feel something they wouldn't otherwise be able to feel. If your process is moving you to genuinely feel something, then the product of that process will show that. That is all you really need to know about being a wealthy artist. When you let go of your intellectual ideas about aesthetics, and hone your process to a point where you can consistently go deep and explore the world beyond your egoic obsessions, it is highly likely that you will sell your work. Other considerations, like your medium, the technology, the scale of your work, your style and presentation – all of that is necessary but secondary, and will come together as a natural part of your process, if you just let it happen and don't try to force it.

Bartering

As a lifelong visual artist and designer who was raised in a Midwestern, lower middle-class neighborhood by parents who worked really hard on a teacher's salary, I have had my struggles with money and with guilt around the idea of making a lot of money. I was also ingrained with the idea, early on, that there was no way in hell I could make a living being an artist. Because of this, for a long time I was forced to get creative with my finances while doing my creative work. What has really saved me in so many situations was the age-old art of bartering. Through the years, I have bartered for rent, for meals, drinks, for extended periods of travel to far-away places, for web hosting, transportation, and many other necessities.

What I've discovered is that most people just want an energy exchange and don't really care about which currency you're using. If you provide value to people, lift their spirits, give them light, and help them to see their circumstances differently, there is no reason you ever need to feel lacking in abundance. And as long as you feel abundant, knowing you have that ability, the money will flow into the cracks where it's needed, and you won't need to worry about where your next meal is coming from.

The Bottom Line

One more thing I want to impress upon you is that, if you want to make a lot of money with your art and buy a big house or a boat, or food for an entire village in Uganda, great – I applaud you. Expand, and give yourself whatever you desire. You really can do it. You might have to learn some marketing skills or get a good coach or agent, but it is entirely doable for you. Though one thing you must never, ever do if your mission is to become a wealthy artist: never stop your flow of creative energy into the world. And never hoard or shut the gilded flood gates of your heart. To pause, and appreciate is great. But never stop showing up and giving yourself. This is the secret to happiness and personal success as an artist, and as a human being.

And if you remember the natural Law of Compensation – you get back what you give – you will never be lacking in any way. You will always be an abundant artist.

CHAPTER
Fourteen

Creating a Body of Work you Feel Good About

– Practical Advice for the Artist

If you hear a voice within you say 'you cannot paint,' then by all means paint, and that voice will be silenced.

— Vincent Van Goh

Dear Artist,

In my experience, by far, the easiest way to create a body of work you feel good about, is to feel good about it as you do it. This might sound like a cheap play on words, but it is one hundred percent true. Of course, that doesn't necessarily mean you need to be blissed out every time you pick up a brush, or a guitar, or your dance shoes. What is important is your ability to give up your ideas about the end result and get lost in your process, getting to a place of confidence and stability of Flow where you don't have to think about it anymore. You just show up every possible day, ideally at the same time, and jump in and let it happen.

The more you are able to just show up and do your work, the better. Make your process ordinary in that way. The less you make a big deal out of it, the easier it will be to drop into your process and float on down the river of creation.

Inspiration, of course, comes when we are relaxed and ready, not when we are uptight and worried about results. In a way, you could say, we don't even really create the end result. The mind thinks we create it, of course, but if you've been working for a while with your medium, you will begin to see things differently. What you will come to understand is that, when you are fully in the flow of your process, you are not really doing the making of the final result – you only see that something is happening, merging, coming together in some way. Then, when you come out of your process, you are able to look at the outcome objectively, as a product of your experience.

Ideally, when we are in our process, we're not going back and forth the whole time, playing artist, then critic, then artist, then critic, which is anathema to your creativity – the analyzing mind is the enemy, not the friend of your creative Flow. This might seem painfully obvious to you, but I have seen so many people try to think their way through their process. They often critique themselves along the way, thinking that it's normal because they never really learned how to get into their Flow.

If you find that your inner critic starts babbling while you're in your process, become aware of it, and do your best to let go of it. The Scuba Training for the Artist practices in Chapter Nine will definitely help with this.

Ultimately, it's good to remember that negative thoughts are only thoughts. They have no bearing on our work until we let them. Once we let a negative thought control our process, we can say 'adios' to a good day's work. When we know that we are the controller and not the victim of our thoughts, we'll have a much easier time staying in our Flow.

Making an Exhibition

Another, more practical way to create a body of work is to set up an exhibition or event somewhere with a deadline, and then work steadily to that deadline. I have personally given myself up to a year to produce a body of work, and that worked well for me. Super tight deadlines can be frustrating, and really long deadlines can be too far ahead to have the right effect. I find that 'not too loose, not too tight' is a good motto for this. Be reasonable and gentle with yourself about this, and take your time. Some of us work better in high energy, high pressure environments, and some of us work better without much pressure or external incentive at all. So find what is best for you and stick with that.

Take time like the river that never grows stale. Keep going and steady. No hurry, no rush.

— Rumi

If you are not able to set up an actual show someplace for whatever reason, you can just make one up. Find a venue that you think would like to have your work, and pretend you're going to have a show there. This is a good way to get the level of your work to where it feels right for you. By creating a body of work with a venue in mind that is a little above your current pay grade, so-to-speak, you can boost your confidence and raise the bar of your work without really thinking about it too much. If you're a painter, and you're showing your work in cafés, create a body of work that will fit nicely in a gallery you like. If you're already showing in a gallery, create a body of work that you can see being accepted into a museum – the MOMA, or whichever one you like. The same goes if you are a musician, or dancer, etc; if your goal is to play better and at bigger venues, practice or choreograph with the intention of performing at those venues.

Just know that when you can stay a little out of your comfort zone with regard to the level or depth of your work, you will push yourself into that level and surprise yourself at what you are capable of. Assign yourself accountability, or get a coach for this – someone who knows what you are capable of, who will support you and steer you in a good direction without being too critical.

One important distinction: I would say, unequivocally, that our goal as artists is to remain in process and let creation happen. I don't believe that is exclusive of pushing ourselves a little. Often where the excitement and passion comes from, is going to places we haven't been before. But please, do not confuse pushing yourself with trying to do something you weren't meant to do, or making something according to a concept or picture you have in your head that doesn't resonate with you when you're in your process. Just remember that whatever picture you have in your mind is a thought; it is not life. With this in mind, please – do not ever compare your work to the work of other artists. Should I repeat this sentence? *Do not compare your work to the work of other artists.* If you make it a point to really grok this, your authenticity will come out, and your work will really shine.

Additionally, as a genuine artist, I would guess that you are more interested in a process of discovery than you are in figuring out how to make things that match your conceptual, critical vocabulary, or preconceived ideas. When I talk about pushing up the bar for yourself, I am talking about feeling, resonating at a certain level, and mastering your medium so you can easily resonate at whatever level you desire. It's not about trying to be someone you're not meant to be, or about struggling to manifest your ideas of perfection. I've been there, I've tried that, and it does not work. Perfectionism has nothing to do with being a real artist, or with being in your Flow – in my experience it will only bring frustration and anxiety, and will make you want to quit making art altogether.

The goal of life is rapture. Art is the way we experience it. Art is the transforming experience.

— Joseph Campbell

Because this is so important, let me reiterate: we cannot create from the heart if we are mentally fixated on an end result. Life does not flow into, or out of, fixed, frozen concepts of good or bad, beautiful or ugly. Life just flows, in the truth of itself, in each moment. We can better hone our process by finding the best way to be able to let go, and let things happen, not by letting our monkey minds get in the way.

The Physical Elements

One crucial element to consider is your environment. If you have not already done so, I strongly encourage you to design the physical elements of your life so that you are inspired to create at the level you want to create. This might mean changing your living area or studio space in some way so that you're excited to be in it, so it's a fun, conducive environment for your process. Making a space that is free from distractions, that feels good to be in, will amp up your ability to stay in your Flow. It is a huge consideration for me personally, for being able to stay in my process and stay focused.

One other thing you may find really helpful is to work alongside other artists. When I lived in a building full of painters and musicians and photographers, I did some of my best work, because we all gave each other creative energy. It was like being carried by an invisible current, and I seemed to literally float on top of it.

I cannot overemphasize this: having friends with similar creative interests near us is invaluable for artists. Imagine lower Manhattan in the 1970s. So many artists who became well-known were living and working in the same neighborhoods – Soho, the East Village, Alphabet City – inspiring and feeding off of each other. Montmartre, Paris, at the turn of the 20th century, during the Belle Époque, is another good, if cliché, example. If you find that you are physically separated from other artists, just keep in touch with them, or make new artist friends wherever you are.

Artist residencies can also be good if you find yourself isolated, because they often involve spaces alongside other artists. However you want to do it, find like souls – all great artists, it seems, maintained close friendships with other artists who influenced them and gave them strength and courage to overcome their creative barriers.

Art Education

This brings me to another important subject – art education. You might have been accepted into a university or art academy that you really liked, and that is great, I applaud you and hope you got a valuable experience out of it. I didn't go to fine art school, and I didn't meet many fine art teachers I liked at the universities I attended, so I went my own way – which was, in retrospect, perfect for me. Though in my early stages as a budding artist, what I really missed was having an art mentor, someone who I looked up to, who could teach me about authenticity and mastering my medium, and the ins and outs of the art world in all its complexity and pitfalls. I learned all of that on my own, and through friends who were other renegade artists who probably learned it from other artists as well.

I cannot stress enough the importance of having a good mentor in some shape or form, who can make your path easier for you – especially in the beginning stages of wresting with your medium. It seems we all need to have someone who has faith in our ability to reach a level higher than we think we can. As I've had many spiritual teachers, I know that they can push us in ways we could never push ourselves. So if we really want to grow as artists and as human beings, mentors are invaluable.

That said, we all have our ways of learning, and art school or no art school, it is crucial to find the support of someone who has already been where we want to go.

To recap, here are some things to remember about creating a body of work you can feel great about:

- Show up every possible day, at a consistent time.

- Hone your process enough to where you can get lost in it.

- Leave your art critic at the door. Critic = death of creativity.

- Remember, thoughts are only thoughts. They have no power over you unless you give them power by believing them.

- Set up a show at a venue, or make up a show, with a reasonable deadline.

- Feel a little above your comfort zone. You can create excitement and energy by knowing you are going someplace you haven't been before.

• Don't compare your work to other artists' work, or to the fantasies in your head.

• Stop trying to 'figure it out.' Stay out of your own way and stay in your Flow, your true home.

• Seek out other like-minded artists.

• Apply for residency programs if that's your thing.

• Find a mentor or art coach, to help you stay in the right direction.

• Have as much fun as humanly possible.

CHAPTER

Fifteen

Landing Clients and Patrons

*If a patron buys from an artist who needs money, the patron then
makes himself equal to the artist. He is building art into the world.
He creates.*

— Ezra Pound

Dear Artist,

Landing art patrons is relatively easy once you have a
body of work you feel good about. You will exude confidence
wherever you go, and people will sense it when you talk about
what you do. I have personally found that selling my work and
getting shows has involved just getting out of the house and
going out to events or clubs and talking to people. If you are
more of an introvert like I am, you can still be effective in the

social scene by showing up and meeting people and being brief but polite by telling them what you do. You don't have to create some kind of artist mystique, or entertain people with stories to get people to support you and buy your work. And you don't have to sell at popular commercial galleries or venues to be successful.

Why People Buy Art

So you might ask, why do people buy art, and why would they buy my art? It's a good question, and the personal insight I will share with you here, about my experience in the visual art world, will shed some light on understanding the minds of your potential patrons, no matter what medium you work in.

When I first started showing my paintings in local galleries, I would of course attend the opening receptions, but acting as if I was another member of the viewing audience – a potential art buyer. It's a funny thing to hear people talk about your work when they are not trying to be nice or agreeable, or when they have had way too many cups of wine and don't really care who they're talking to. What I discovered was that there is no one psychology to it – everyone had a different point of view about liking or disliking a piece. And each person had their own completely unique reasons for wanting to buy or not buy. Some people said they had an empty spot on the wall above their couch; some had a relative they thought might like it; others had just bought a new house and wanted to fill it up with the art of one of their friends, or friends of friends. Some people, it seemed, just wanted to buy when they saw other people buying.

What was also interesting is that I had my own niche of people who bought my art, and most of them were either acquaintances of mine, or friends of acquaintances. Most people liked to know who the artist was they were buying from, and they liked to know that they weren't the only one buying from that artist.

Find Your People

As there are, these days, as many different ways to sell one's work as there are artists selling work, I won't mention too many specific methods here. In my experience, the most time and energy you'll put into showing your work, is in finding the people who are most likely to buy your work. Then you can make a game plan and work out the details on how you want to approach them or invite them. Remember, your confidence and communication skills are everything to these people.

You will, most of the time, end up selling to people who are comfortable around you. I am guessing you are not a salesperson, so it's probably best to let your work speak for itself. Consider that many patrons secretly want to be artists themselves, so just being confident and letting your work sell itself is enough.

One way to approach this is to hang out where those people are and just be yourself, and let them know what you do.

This might sound terrifying to some artists who don't like to socialize much, and I get that. But there are many ways to get people's attention, and you will find your method with a little experimentation.

I have often found that getting into group shows is good for this, but even better is just to have your own show or exhibition (or with one or two other artists) someplace that you know your people will show up, with a little effort at getting the word out. Once you get good at letting the right people know about you, make sure you keep a book of contact information of all your potential patrons – and especially of people who have already bought from you. You can write them a postcard or send an email every few months, letting them know what you're up to, or giving them the date of your next show. Just keep it simple and don't overdo this part – less is more, in terms of keeping people in the loop.

Another way that works well for selling directly to people is to invite them to your studio. It seems obvious, but I didn't catch on to this idea until I saw a friend of mine doing it, and it really works. Just find people who you know are art collectors or philanthropists and call them up or email them and ask them to come for a visit. You might be surprised at how much people like to visit to a studio, and buy directly from an artist.

You can also make connections by finding the people who select the visual art for buildings of larger companies. I have gotten my biggest commissions by getting in the door of companies through some other avenue, and meeting the people who make the creative decisions there. Once you meet and befriend these people, mention what you do, or take them out to lunch and ask them questions about their work. Just be vulnerable, and let them see what you do. You can also ask them who their decorator is, and contact the decorator directly. Or if you know someone in the company, even better. You can just ask them to direct you to the right person, along with their recommendation of you. Then set up an appointment with that new contact and make a presentation to them in person, letting them know other people you sell to that they might recognize.

The key here is that people should know your work is already out there, even in some minor way, in a blog or magazine article, or on so-and-so's walls, or in a local gallery. People often want art that they know other people like, including their friends, because, oddly, many art buyers really only want to buy what is popular, and will routinely defer to other people they know who have strong opinions or knowledge about what is in fashion. So, the more you can connect your work to someone or something they already know and like, the better. (If you are in the beginning stages of showing your work, you can always find friends' places to show in – even if it's just in their house – and then build up your exhibition experience from there.)

Other Avenues for Finding and Keeping Art Patrons

• *Writing letters.* One particular method I will mention here, because I think it's quite good, is writing letters. You can work miracles this way. Find people who you know have given to art projects similar to yours, and how much they usually give, and write them a nice, handwritten letter. Don't be afraid to ask for a donation for your project or upcoming body of work, knowing what they are likely to give based on your research on them. Or use the letter to set up a meeting with them to present your work. The last thing people are going to expect is a well-researched, handwritten letter, so make it impressive. Your sincerity and inventiveness will get you very far, and they will respect you for reaching out in such a creative and thoughtful way.

• *Having an exhibition or event at a popular gallery or venue.* This is ideal for a lot of artists, and if you can find a gallery that will accept your work and keep you on as a regular showing artist, more power to you. But it has its drawbacks, one of which is that you'll usually end up with only 50% of your sales, and no contacts for repeat patrons.

• *Having an exhibition or event in other places.* Find out where art patron-type people go and then make a plan to show your work there. It could be a doctor's office, a local theatre, a nice hotel, or somewhere else where the style of your work will fit nicely.

• *Showing your work in cafés.* I wouldn't even think about it if you're at all serious about selling your work. People do not go to cafés to buy art. They go to drink coffee.

• *Online Venues.* If you decide the in-person route to selling your work is not for you, you can always go through the internet to reach people. Many artists have done this successfully, and it just takes getting to know the venue site and making sure your people are already buying from there.

• *Crowd funding online.* Crowdfunding, through Indiegogo or other sites, continues to work well for many artists, especially if you like to make books of your art, or small items you can inexpensively replicate, that you can give away to people who fund your project. This is also a good way to just get the word out about what you do.

There are a thousand other ways to attract the people who will buy from you, and thinking out of the box will certainly help this process. The important thing is to go about it in a way that you're comfortable with and that's fun for you.

In the end, whichever way you decide to sell your work, remember that people often want to buy because they respect the arts and want to be a part of it. There are many art enthusiasts who don't know how to be creative with the exception of their pocketbooks – so you are giving them an opportunity to participate in something they really care about. You are creating value for them, just by letting them in on the art game.

CHAPTER
Sixteen

Obstacles to your Art Dreams

If you can find a path with no obstacles, it probably doesn't lead anywhere.

— Frank A. Clark

Dear Artist,

By now, you should have a good idea about what to expect if you decide to take the plunge and follow your art to new depths. One thing I can promise you is that your journey will not be boring. You will have obstacles, and bumps in the road, and that will make it even more exciting and more worth doing, because there is so much to learn. One day you might look back at your life and see the changes you've made in the world, and feel a great sense of accomplishment, a recognition that you did the impossible.

And there will be times when you will experience feeling like you aren't getting anywhere. We are all set in our ways, and often it can seem impossible to shed old habit patterns to adopt new ones. Chances are you will struggle with applying one or more of the principles in this book to your own life, because it is just too damn difficult. This is when it's good to enlist the help of a mentor or coach who is familiar with the path, who can hold you accountable for your process and make the tough spots easier. It's like having a knowledgable tour guide vs. just reading the placards. You'll develop faster, and you will have a greater rate of success.

The Potholes

Have no fear of perfection – you'll never reach it.

— Salvador Dali

Additionally, I have found it's much easier to stay positive about the perils of an adventure when you have a roadmap of the potholes. So I've made a list of some of the common obstacles, along with their antidotes, that have been known to show up for artists on their journey.

- It seems too difficult to do my art. There are so many forces against me. *It's not too difficult if you take it one day, and one moment, at a time. Plan every day out on a calendar, and be realistic with how much you can do. And make your process fun.*

• I get too emotional, I feel overwhelmed when I do my work. *This will change. You'll feel more balanced as you keep going with your process and become more accustomed to it. And if you work with a compassionate attitude – not just thinking about yourself – it will take a lot of the pressure off.*

• I don't have enough time after my day job to do my creative process. And my friends and family don't give me enough time or personal space for it. *Remember this: "Time is a created thing. To say 'I don't have time', is like saying, 'I don't want to.'" — Lao Tzu. Shorten your work week, if at all possible, and schedule in time to do your creative work. You will have more time when you make more time. And don't give in to distraction – turn off your devices, and lock your door.*

• I don't have the discipline to keep going. *Again, this is where planning comes in. If you stick to the plan, discipline is not an issue. You just do it because it's on the schedule.*

• My parents, or my family, don't support me enough. *Your family is not responsible for supporting you. You are responsible for supporting you, for knowing your own needs, and for loving yourself and your purpose enough to make it happen, one way or another.*

• I will probably lose interest and end up doing what I always do, which is nothing. *Make an internal commitment, and get a mentor or coach. Find artist friends to encourage and inspire you.*

• I might lose hope that making a living from my art is even possible. *You won't lose hope if you have someone to guide you. Find that person who you can rely on for help, such as a coach or teacher. Find, or make friends who are already making a living with their art.*

• I have no job security as an artist. *'Job security' is an illusion. If you are eating, and have a roof over your head, and you're happily painting or playing music all day, who cares about job security? You are doing what you were meant to do. Nothing is more real and more deeply rewarding than that. And if you decide to make a lot of money from your work, then you can do that too!*

• There are so many other artists that are better than me. Why even try? *There will always be better, and worse, artists than you. The point is not to be the best, although you can strive for that if it helps to give you discipline. The point is to live a happy life where you're doing, every day, what it is that you love to do.*

• I never really like what I create, or, I just can't seem to get it perfect. *Keep creating. You will be amazed that, as you let go deeper into your process, and as you have more fun with it, the results will get better. Remember that perfectionism kills creativity and takes the fun out of your process – so stay with it, and let go of thinking about the results as much as you can.*

Whatever you come up against, just know that if you have confidence in yourself and in your process, and you persevere, you will succeed in converting the potholes into opportunities. You'll make problems into subject matter, or emotional drive, that will inspire and sustain your process. This is one great advantage to being a working artist – everything is available to you. Life, with all its ups and downs, likes and dislikes, ease and dis-ease, is your process – nothing is outside of your reach for what you can incorporate into the creative Flow. This, for me, is what makes being an artist so much fun, and so liberating. We don't have to reject anything – we can learn to feel and transform any experience. If we dive into our Flow and stay there for awhile, it becomes apparent that the world is truly our canvas. It is our music, our dance, our performance. It is what we desire it to be.

What I've found is that when we keep going despite the apparent obstacles, we will find our truth. And our truth is the one that matters – it is our divine gift to the world.

CHAPTER

Seventeen

What Now?

Life is a series of natural and spontaneous changes. Don't resist them, that only creates sorrow. Let reality be reality. Let things flow naturally forward in whatever way they like.

— Lao Tzu

Dear Artist,

There have been many times when I was forced to make compromises with my creative goals. The challenges I faced, the many obstacles, and frustrations, seemed at the time like they were just keeping me from doing my true purpose. In retrospect, I can see that it was all part of something much bigger than myself – that the valuable lessons I learned over the years are not just for me, they're also for you.

So if you decide that you want to quit your job and do your art full time, the information in this book will help you. If you decide you want to evolve your creative process to another level, to do what you love while keeping a day job or doing other projects, this book gives you the tools to do it.

My greatest wish for you is just that you get nothing short of what you truly desire, because what you desire is absolutely valid and doable. If you can imagine it, believe in it, and commit to it, there is nothing stopping you. Just go at your own pace, and do your best to stay on your path when the changes and challenges come up. If you keep showing up to do your work, without worrying about the results, about what other people think, or what your inner critic thinks – the results will be monumental.

~ Finis ~

If you want to inquire about coaching with Douglas, or just have a question, feel free to contact him at this email:
info@divinecreativity.org

To inquire about creativity workshops and
artist development classes, go to: *divinecreativity.org*

Bibliography

Foreward

T.S. Eliot. "The Waste Land," https://www.poetryfoundation.org/poems/47311/the-waste-land

Chapter 4

Joseph Campbell. "Joseph Campbell and the Power of Myth." Interview with Bill Moyers, Mystic Fire Video, 1997.

Terence McKenna. "No Guru, No Method, No Teacher." Lecture, Esalen Institute, August 1993.

Albert Einstein. "Letters of Note," *The Delusion, Nov. 10, 2011. http://www.lettersofnote.com/2011/11/delusion.html*

Chapter 5

Matthew Fox. *Creativity,* (New York: Penguin/Tarcher, June 17, 2004).

Encyclopedia of Art and Classical Antiquities. "Ancient Greek Sculpture." http://www.visual-arts-cork.com/antiquity/sculpture-ancient-greece.htm

Mao Zedong. Wikipedia: "Art for Art's Sake," https://en.wikipedia.org/wiki/Art_for_art%27s_sake

Chapter 6

Alan Watts. "Life is Magic," Alan Watts recordings - http://www.alanwatts.org/

Chögyam Trungpa. *True Perception and the Path of Dharma Art,* (Boston, MA: Shambhala Publications, Inc., 1994).

Joseph Campbell. "Joseph Campbell and the Power of Myth." Interview with Bill Moyers, Mystic Fire Video, 1997.

Chapter 8

Julia Cameron. *The Artist's Way: a spiritual path to higher creativity*, (New York: Tarcher/Putnam, 1992).

"Famous People Who Meditate," https://www.ranker.com/list/celebrities-who-meditate/celebrity-lists

"5 Famous Artists That Meditate," http://rubinmuseum.org/blog/5-famous-artists-that-meditate

Joseph Campbell. "Joseph Campbell and the Power of Myth." Interview with Bill Moyers, Mystic Fire Video, 1988.

Chögyam Trungpa. *True Perception and the Path of Dharma Art*, (Boston, MA: Shambhala Publications, Inc., 1994).

Chapter 9

Sensei Yuko Halada teaches private one on one calligraphy lessons in Phoenix Arizona. Yukolove.com.

Chapter 10

"Online Oxford English Dictionary," *https://en.oxforddictionaries.com/definition/discipline*

Chapter 11

Jim Jarmusch. "Things I've learned," *https://www.moviemaker.com/archives/series/things_learned/jim-jarmusch-5-golden-rules-of-moviemaking/* Accessed: 9/20/2018

Matthew Silver. Who is Matthew Silver? Legendary NYC Street Performer, (Youtube, 2017).

Lester Levenson. *http://www.lesterlevenson.org/audio-video.php*

Leonard Cohen. "How to Speak Poetry," *Death of a Lady's Man.* (London: Andre Deutsch; Reprint edition, May 1, 2011).

Chapter 12

Caroline Myss. "Transending the Tribe." https://www.personalgrowthcourses.net/stories/myss.relationship_transcending_tribe

Alan Watts. "Playing the Game of Life," (Excerpt from Alan Watts' speech) *https://genius.com/Alan-watts-playing-the-game-of-life-annotated*

Bentinho Massaro. "Home to the sincere and committed spiritual practitioner," *http://www.bentinhomassaro.tv*

Teal Swan. "How to find a core belief," *https://tealswan.com/resources/articles/how-to-find-a-core-belief/*

Acknowledgments

Since it would take up the whole book to mention all of the beautiful humans who in some way contributed to the ideas in this book, I will keep this list short.

Thank you –

To my teachers who have passed on: Lester Levenson, Chögyam Trungpa Rinpoche, Rev. Pat Hawk, John Daido Loori, Rev. George Bailey. To my teachers and friends still living: Sarvi, Brian Smith and Cindy Lee, John Yates, Geshe Jinpa Sonam, Zoketsu Norman Fischer, Yoshi Nakano, Yuko Halada, Steven and Ann Saitzik, David Hurwith and Mirah Love, Shastri Alexander deVaron, Terry Tapp, Tom Clark, Shane and Meaghan Carpenter, Dmitriy Yepishin, Morgan and Tammy Adrian, Paula Maas and Martin Turner, Will Duncan and Ann Curry, Devora Maché, Jacqueline Fisher. To my parents, Dennis and Marie Smith, and my sister Julie Smith; my grandparents who have passed on, Paul and Ethel Smith, and Julia Miner. Animals: Stanley Wayne Smith, Bubbs, and Lucie. Thank you, also, to my editors — Marion Meister, Bets Greer, Edward Levy, Jen Tan, Amy Wallace, and to Ora, Cheyenne Giesecke, and Angela Lauria for their help on the prewriting stages. And finally, Thank you to all who helped with my book launch – Bets Greer, Elizabeth Burnett, Paula Maas, Gulnara Gulchick, David Beaubien, Andreana Karabotsios, Brian Maite, Irma Gomez, Sarah Mann, Bliss Griffin Rowland, and anyone else I failed to mention who helped with the book.

Quote Overflow

"You want to be popular? It's easy to do. Just be a total weirdo and love yourself for it." — Dan Pearce

The difficulty lies not so much in developing new ideas as in escaping from old ones. — John Maynard Keynes

To pay attention, this is our endless and proper work. — Mary Oliver

We need more people speaking out. This country is not overrun with rebels and free thinkers. It's overrun with sheep and conformists. — Bill Maher

It is only with the heart that one can see rightly; what is essential is invisible to the eye. — Antoine de St. Exupery

Art that cannot shape society and therefore also cannot penetrate the heart questions of society, [...] is no art. — Joseph Beuys 1985

Further Reading

The War of Art, by Steven Pressfield

The Artist's Way, by Julia Cameron

True Perception: The Path of Dharma Art, by Chögyam Trungpa

Creativity, by Matthew Fox

The Power of Myth, by Joseph Campbell

The Artist as Culture Producer, edited by Sharon Louden

Launching Your Art Career: A Practical Guide for Artists, by Alix Sloan

Super Accelerated Living, by Bentinho Massaro

The Mind Illuminated, by Culadasa

Death of a Lady's Man, by Leonard Cohen

Fund Your Dreams Like a Creative Genius: A Guide for Artists, Entrepreneurs, Inventors, and Kindred Spirits, by Brainard Carey

On finding and changing limiting beliefs:

Bentinho Masaro: *Home to the sincere and committed spiritual practitioner. http://www.bentinhomassaro.tv*

Teal Swan: *How to Find a Core Belief. https://tealswan.com/ resources/articles/how-to-find-a-core-belief*

About the Author

Douglas Paul Smith is the founder of Divine Creativity Productions, and The Artist Coach – which empowers artists to reach personal success through their individual creative process. His passion for coaching artists was born from a decade of teaching 'Art As Meditation' classes – his own version of the millennia-old Eastern principles of creativity as taught by the late Chögyam Trungpa in the 70s and 80s. He also studied Yogic philosophy and Meditation extensively in the traditions of Tibetan Gelugpa, Shambhala, and Zen Buddhism, and is formally trained as a Contemplative Arts Instructor at Shambhala Art International, in Los Angeles.

Douglas' own work as a painter and illustrator spans decades, his style consistently reminiscent of primitive art and children's drawings. Having thrown out all technical conventions from his design training, Douglas' work demonstrates a Basquiat-like focus on the immediacy and innocence of the unlearned hand. The flavor of much of his work stems from his fascination with Buddhism and meditative development of the mind, as well as a life-long interest in the stratums of sense perceptions and emotions that connect the mind, body, and spirit.

Douglas is currently painting, designing, and coaching other Artists. He lives in southern California.